MW01487572

"First Reconciliation an Living Forgiveness is a r cry, nod your head, and again. Learning what it means to be forgiven and to forgive is paramount for any person. The McGradys approach this topic with such love, care, compassion, and, when appropriate, lightheartedness. First Reconciliation isn't just for the kids! It's for each of us in the Church, and we hope that this book will become a staple for every family and person involved with sacramental prep and beyond."

Jason and Rachel Bulman
National speakers and hosts of *Meet the Bulmans*

"With unrivaled wit and authenticity, Tommy and Katie speak into the fears and misconceptions that keep too many Catholics away from God's amazing sacrament of peace, joy, love, healing, and spiritual freedom! As a resource for themselves and their children, parents will find this book delightfully practical, personable, and prayerful."

Sr. Mary Michael Fox, OP
Author of *Following God's Pedagogy: Principles for Children's Catechesis*

"What a gift this is for families! Thank you, McGradys, for tackling a subject that has too infrequently been written about in a digestible way for families, especially parents who may not have a healthy relationship with Confession themselves. This book is a wonderful help for parish and classroom sacramental formation programs because it centers the irreplaceable role of parents and family life in understanding the fruits of this sacrament—the graces of mercy, forgiveness, and reconciliation.

Parents, if you are going to read one thing to help establish your home as a place of forgiveness and mercy, this is the book for you! It will prepare you and your children for not only their First Reconciliation but every reception of the sacrament thereafter."

Katherine Bogner
Teacher, catechist, and author of *Through the Year with Jesus* and *All about Lent & Holy Week*

"Tommy and Katie McGrady provide helpful, easy-to-read, and deeply insightful guidance for parents helping their children prepare for receiving God's love and mercy in the Sacrament of Reconciliation. With their wonderful kids, the McGradys have impeccable credentials! Down-to-earth and filled with relatable real-life stories, *First Reconciliation and Beyond* can help inspire a renewed love in all of us for this beautiful sacrament!"

Cardinal Timothy M. Dolan
Archbishop of New York

First
Reconciliation
and Beyond

A Family's Guide for Learning and Living Forgiveness

Tommy *and* Katie McGrady
Hosts of Family Mass Prep on Hallow

AVE MARIA PRESS AVE Notre Dame, Indiana

Nihil Obstat: Reverend Monsignor Michael Heintz, PhD
                    Censor Librorum

Imprimatur: Most Reverend Kevin C. Rhoades
                    Bishop of Fort Wayne–South Bend
                    Given at Fort Wayne, Indiana, on May 21, 2025

Founded in 1865, Ave Maria Press is a ministry of the United States Province of Holy Cross.

www.avemariapress.com

Paperback: ISBN-13 978-1-64680-415-3

E-book: ISBN-13 978-1-64680-416-0

Cover image © Getty Images

Cover design by Brianna Dombo and Christopher D. Tobin.

Text design by Christopher D. Tobin.

Printed and bound in the United States of America.

Library of Congress Cataloging-in-Publication Data is available.

—

To the St. Margaret Catholic School community,
especially the class of 2031.
We are grateful for your inspiring witness to the perfect mercy
and abundant love of the Father.

Contents

Prologue

In the Beginning

Katie: A New Moment

I walked into the living room and my daughter, five and a half at the time, quickly hit the "off" button on the TV remote control. I could tell she'd had something on the screen she probably didn't have permission to watch, but I didn't know what. In an instant, I knew how I handled the next interaction would be pivotal in our relationship.

"Bud, what were you watching?" I asked.

"Nothing," she quickly fired back.

"Are you sure?" I pressed.

"Yes," she said, refusing to make eye contact.

I sighed. You know the one. The "I know you probably aren't telling me the truth, and I want you to know that I know" sigh. The one that indicates what every child dreads, a parent declaring, "I'm not mad. I'm just disappointed." We've all been on the receiving end of this sigh as children, and it's not much better being on the delivery end of this sigh as a parent.

I calmly said to my child, "Well, when you're ready to tell me what was on the TV screen, you let me know," and I walked into the kitchen, my heart pounding, my hands clammy, my mind spinning. Never had I been so stressed as a parent, or worried I'd handle an interaction well. Because I knew, in that moment, having caught my child actively doing the wrong thing and then not being totally honest about it, that we were crossing a threshold. Gone were the bouncing baby, the wobbly toddler, and even the joyful little girl who still couldn't fully pronounce her *R*s. Now I had a child, sitting in the other room, who was lying to me after she'd done the wrong thing, and I wasn't fully prepared for it.

Sure, we'd disciplined her before. She'd had her fair share of time-outs, and then, in the three weeks we'd tried (and largely failed) to be gentle parents, we'd done an equal measure of "Let's talk about our feelings." There had been more than enough corrections and redirections. We were far from laissez-faire parents. But we hadn't come to this moment yet, the one when our child would choose the wrong thing, know she'd done wrong, and then not want to admit it to us.

I stood in the kitchen, my mind racing. Her little sister was taking a nap. My husband was still at work. It was just me, at this moment, with a lying child in the other room who likely knew I knew that she'd lied.

I counted to ten, just as her dad and I had taught her to do when she was upset. The *Daniel Tiger's Neighborhood* jingle played in my head. I certainly was feeling so mad that I wanted to roar. But my anger was coupled with sadness and fear. I was upset she didn't think she could tell me she'd made a mistake and a bad choice. I was fearful this was the start of years of dishonesty and deception. And I was angry, most especially that now I would probably have to enact a strict punishment to try to prevent this from happening again. But ultimately, I didn't quite know *what* to do. How do you enact a punishment that is just but also merciful? How do you not overreact or underreact? What could this do to our relationship in the future?

As I counted and thought, standing in the kitchen racking my brain for what to do next, my daughter walked into the kitchen, her head hung low. I could see tears begin to well up in her eyes. Her voice shook as she quietly said, "Mom, I was on YouTube." And then she began to sob.

I stood there, gobsmacked and more than a little relieved, as she sobbed her way through her explanation. She'd been watching a show on Disney (one she was allowed to watch and had seen many times before), and when it ended, she wanted to find a video about one of the characters that we'd all watched on YouTube before. She'd opened up the app on the TV but didn't know how to find the search function or spell the character's name, and so she just started clicking around. Another video had started playing, and long story longer, she was trying to get off of YouTube when I'd walked into the living room, so she panicked and just turned the TV off.

The words fell out of her mouth. Her cheeks were red, her voice unsteady, and the tears seemed to come from the depths of her little body that was clearly racked with guilt and shame. She knew she'd made a mistake, both going onto YouTube and then lying about it, and she expressed nothing but remorse. I think she spent more time confessing her crime than the amount of time she was even on YouTube.

She finally came up for air in the midst of her explanation, but before I could say anything in response, I noticed she was holding the TV remote in her hand. She lifted her arm, held out her hand, and offered the remote to me. "Mom, I shouldn't be allowed to watch TV the rest of the day. I'm going to my room, and I'm so sorry." Off she walked, her head practically touching her stomach, the tears still flowing down her little face.

I gave her a few moments alone in her bedroom, her sobs echoing down the hall. When I finally walked in, I found her sitting on her bed, curled up under her favorite blanket, clutching a stuffie, the saddest I think I'd ever seen her. So, I sat down on the edge of her bed and just pulled her in for a hug, letting her cry for a few more minutes.

I hadn't said a word after her confession, and yet here she was, upset not because she'd been punished, but because she'd broken a rule, lied about it, and then admitted her mistake. Her sadness stemmed entirely from her sense of shame, as she was clearly horrified that she'd done something terrible. I marveled at the moment, silent simply from the shock and quickness of it all. All of it was a snapshot of a profound human experience, wrapped up in a little girl who had never experienced these actions and emotions all at once before. And as I held her in that grace-filled moment that comes when one finds herself in the thick of living her vocation, I heard, "This is how I hold you." And then I began to cry.

Tommy: No Dessert

For the first few years of Rose's life, she was (and still is), to Katie and me, a slice of heaven coming to dwell in our hearts and home. Through the exhaustion and frustrations of new parenthood, we did our level best to instill virtues into our little girl. We encouraged and rewarded her development of kindness, sharing, and caring. Her mistakes were innocent and correctable. We looked with pride at how she interacted with her peers and forged her first friendships. She was, it seemed, to be as perfect a child as a child can be. And then came the incident that Katie just shared.

When Katie texted to fill me in, we decided: no dessert that night. A just punishment, although heavy for a little kid to reckon with. I do believe if you check the latest version of the parental punishment pamphlet, we were well within the sentencing guidelines. I began to feel the gravity of the moment I would face when I came home from work.

Parents craft the lenses through which their children will view the world. That sentiment alone is worth a fair number of sleepless nights and its own patch of gray hair. As daunting as this responsibility is, it is surely magnified and multiplied when we begin to comprehend that we also craft the lenses through which our children will encounter and understand God. With this understanding in the background, I decided to use how upset she was about disappointing us, as well as about not getting to have dessert, as a teachable moment about sin, mercy, grace, and forgiveness.

I got home from work and found Rose in her room, sitting timidly on her bed next to her pillows and stuffies, damp with tears. I asked her what had happened, and I listened as she explained the *whats* and the *whys*. I had her tell me what the punishment was: no ice cream. I reinforced how serious it is to lie to Mommy and Daddy and how important trust is in our relationship. Then I tried to shift things. "Rose," I said, "because I love you, I will take the punishment for you. After dinner, you will stay with Mommy and Clare, and I will go to your room until everyone has finished their dessert."

Rose was relieved and grateful, but now she was upset that I wouldn't be able to enjoy ice cream with everyone else because of her choices. As we hugged and she cried, we talked about how we all make mistakes like this—we sin against one another and against God. The wrong has been done, and when we do wrong, we feel it deep down in our souls. We feel the guilt and sorrow, which are the burdens of our sin. But Jesus loves us so much that he took the guilt and sorrow; the pain and the burden of our sins with him when he died on the Cross. That sacrifice of love made it possible for us to be freed of our sins. In Jesus and in his love that we share with one another, we find mercy, forgiveness, and love everlasting.

Perhaps reading this, your instinct is to think we were being softies, letting her "get away" with the lie, since the only punishment or consequence for my daughter's sin was *me* not having some cookie dough crunch with the family that evening. But there was something deeper I wanted to show in that moment, a lesson to be learned. It isn't about "break a rule, get punished." Life is long, and there will be plenty of doing wrong and consequent punishments over the years, no doubt. But this was a chance to illustrate the love of a father and try to show her the real meaning of forgiveness, reconciliation, and loving mercy.

How God Holds Us

In those initial moments of our daughter's mistake, confession, and then deep shame, we ran through the gamut of parental emotions. We were initially frustrated and angry, ready to dole out justice, but then shocked into silence when she seemed prepared to punish herself. Then, we both realized, we had each gone through this same cycle, again and again, not with our own parents when we were young, but in the confessional, where we admit and take responsibility for our sins. Because of the grace of the Sacrament of Reconciliation (or Penance) and the gift of the ministry of the Church, we are held close and loved as we are assured of the Lord's forgiveness and his loving mercy.

We see our little ones with love and pride, hoping to hold them close for as long as we have them. But helping them accept responsibility for correcting their wrongs, deciding on consequences for their misbehaviors, and guiding them back to the right path is hard! It is our responsibility to navigate their little hearts and growing minds and to do so with sensitivity and kindness. It's a sacred duty.

These parental responsibilities and the feelings they stir in us give us tiny glimpses into the love of God for us—his beloved, imperfect, and sometimes sinful children. At times we are the child who has chosen to do the wrong thing, and sometimes our sense of shame and sadness at our sin drives us to confess the wrong and punish ourselves to the extreme. Sometimes we are the child who has willfully misbehaved, and we are obstinate, refusing to admit we've done anything wrong, running from an honest admission of our wrongdoing. Other times, we're so frequently choosing the wrong things that we don't even realize we have something to confess at all, because the sin has become familiar, comfortable, and entirely normal in our lives.

Yet wherever we are, in whatever state we find ourselves, God longs to hold us close. This is perhaps the only frame of mind that works, or is remotely helpful, when thinking about the Sacrament of Reconciliation. God doesn't just wait around to catch us doing wrong. Rather, God invites us to come to him and tell him what we have done, honestly confess our mistakes, and resolve to not do it again, with the help of his grace. We receive his grace because God holds us close, letting us lean into him, sometimes sobbing, sometimes obstinate, sometimes fearful that he won't want to hold us, and sometimes thinking he is so far away that his arms don't seem big or wide enough to scoop us up. But that's the gift of God's mercy, compassion, and abundant love: Our sins are never too scary, our sobs are never too loud, and our failures are never too big.

We have all been either the child who has made the mistake or the adult on the receiving end of the confession of said mistake, and so experiencing mercy, imparting justice, and understanding the collection of feelings is a fundamental part of the human experience. As Catholics, the Sacrament of Reconciliation is an intense distillation of that human experience. In the sanctity of the confessional, again and again, we are offered mercy, forgiveness, and a chance to heal. When we prepare for Reconciliation, whether for the first time or throughout our lives, we are preparing ourselves to be held close by the Lord. We should take it seriously, but also recognize the joy in it all—namely, that we can be held close, even when we have stumbled and fallen. Perhaps where we have fallen is right into the arms of the merciful God who loves us.

This book is meant to be a help, for both you and the child(ren) in your life preparing for this sacrament, to more fully understand, appreciate, and lean into being held by God through the Sacrament of Reconciliation. It's the book we were looking for as we helped our own child get ready to go to Confession for the first time. As she expressed her worries or doubts, as she asked questions about what would happen or how it worked, and as she bounced out of the confessional with the biggest smile, this was the book we wanted to create to help others who would walk that same road. We hope the reflections on scripture, the conversation starters, the hopefully relatable stories, and the quick guide to Confession at the end will help you more deeply recognize the great gift of Reconciliation and better prepare yourself and your little ones for this sacrament.

Using This Book

The first step we urge is for you to download and print for easy reference (and a handy bookmark) a copy of *The Order for Reconciling Individual Penitents* made available by the Federation of Diocesan Liturgical Commissions (FDLC) found by scanning the QR code or visiting tinyurl.com/orderofpenance.

Each chapter offers you five parts or faith-growing habits that we have found helpful for our family. The first two habits are essentially about learning through story, ours and the Church's, and the remaining three habits are practical applications of the stories' lessons. Revisit these chapters and faith-growing habits often as you and your child continue to grow closer to God as you prepare for and well beyond the celebration of his or her First Reconciliation.

1. **Joining Our Stories to the Church's Story:** The opening of each chapter is a true story from our lives that we have found instructive as we continue our own formation and learn how to form our daughters in our Catholic faith. We try to link for you our story with that of the spiritual and sacramental Tradition—or story—of the Catholic Church so that you can learn to see your story within the faith Tradition of the Church as well.

2. **Learning from Scripture:** In this part of each chapter, we take you through a passage from the Bible that we find helpful in making sense of the Sacrament of Reconciliation and provide parent-friendly commentary about its meaning in contemporary life.

3. **Thinking and Growing as Parents:** Here we offer some food for thought by way of reflection or conversation questions to help you grow as an adult and a parent in your own understanding of the message and lessons of the scripture passage explored in the previous part.

4. **Growing Together as Parents and Children:** In this part, we provide some guidance and a sample script for reflecting and talking with your child about the scripture passage and how it can help all of us understand the Sacrament of Reconciliation better.

5. **Praying as a Family:** Here we make a few suggestions about how to pray together through the time of preparing your child for First Reconciliation and beyond. This need not be fancy or complicated, and we hope our pointers help.

In the appendix you will find a list of scripture passages that can help you prepare for going to Confession as well as three examinations of conscience to help you and your child consider what wrongdoing or sins you have done. There is one for adults, one for children, and a third for families to use together. Lastly, use the FDLC printout mentioned

previously as you make your way through this book. It will also be
helpful for those of you who might be returning to Confession for the
first time in a long while.

Take notes in the margins, underline or highlight, or do whatever
will help you feel at home as you read this book.

From Our Family to Yours

We wrote this book in real time as we helped our eldest daughter, Rose,
prepare for her First Reconciliation. As she prepared, we prepared,
too, and something beautiful happened in our family. We came to see
the great gift of the Sacrament of Reconciliation as a foundation and
a launchpad to joy and holiness for our family. As she examined her
conscience, we examined ours. As she learned to apologize or forgive
more quickly, and fervently, so did we. As she came to understand what
mercy and forgiveness look like and sought it in the confessional, we
came to see mercy and forgiveness more clearly, too, especially in our
home. The entire time we were reminded just how *new* we are to raising
kids in the faith and parenting. If anything, writing this book kept us
grounded in the fact that most parents, at all stages, are figuring it out
as they go along. We offer you our stories, heartfelt encouragement,
and bits of advice with the huge caveat that we, just like you, are still
learning how to be good Catholic parents.

Get in Line

Joining Our Stories to the Church's Story

Katie: You Can't Go Wrong

After a wild day and a half of travel, with nine teenagers in tow, we finally arrived in Rome and headed straight for St. Peter's Basilica. It's always the first stop on a trip to the Eternal City, and we wanted to head over to try to catch the sunset from the square. The security line moved rather quickly, and even though we were all tired and could use a shower after more than twenty-four hours of airports and flying, we were all thrilled to be at the heart of the Church.

As we walked in, instantly captivated by Bernini's gilded canopy above the main altar and Michelangelo's *Pieta*, the stunning marble statue of Mary holding Jesus's body just taken down from the Cross, one of the young men in the group asked me if Confessions were available in St. Peter's. "Oh they're available, in practically every language you can imagine!" and I pointed in the direction of the confessionals lined up on the right-hand side of St. Peter's Basilica.

There must be at least twenty of them, these tiny, wooden, free-standing confessionals, with a priest sitting in the center. You can kneel on the side, sort of shoving yourself into the corner so you can confess your sins anonymously, behind the screen, or you can kneel in front of the priest, face-to-face with your confessor. Red and green lights toggle on and off, letting the people in line know when it's their turn, and as you kneel down at this tiny box in this colossal church that holds the graves of saints and popes, you can't help but feel deeply connected to the depth, breadth, history, and meaning of our Church.

My student traipsed off to the confessionals, excited to go to Reconciliation in St. Peter's. As he walked off, something stirred inside me. "Maybe I should go, too," a little voice said in my head. We'd call this my conscience, wouldn't we? That still, small voice that guides me, helps me choose right from wrong, keeps me tethered to what is true and beautiful. Then that little voice said, "But I want to walk around and see everything." "Can't you walk around while going to the confessionals?" My conscience seemed in conflict with itself.

Then, as if the dove in the Holy Spirit window at the back of St. Peter's flew down and landed on my shoulder, the nudge to just go back to the confessionals and go to Reconciliation became very strong. My feet started moving, and the next thing I knew, I found myself standing in line, the tiny confessionals lined up before me. It felt right.

I do the same thing every time I find myself standing in the Confession line: I take a couple of deep breaths, try to clear my head, and then begin working my way down the list of the Ten Commandments. It's how Mrs. Tartamella taught me to make an examination of conscience many years ago, in the fall of second grade.

1. *You shall have no other gods before me.* What have I made an idol in my life?

2. *You shall not take the Lord's name in vain.* When have I cursed and disrespected God's holy name?

3. *You shall keep holy the sabbath day.* Have I skipped Sunday Mass, avoided prayer, or kept God at a distance?

As I was making my way down the list, asking myself fairly standard, boilerplate questions to examine my conscience, I found myself looking around at St. Peter's Basilica, captivated by the place and feeling tiny.

"Katie?" I heard my name and quickly turned around, expecting to see one of the students on the pilgrimage looking for me. But standing there, two people behind me in the Confession line at St. Peter's Basilica, on a random afternoon in June 2013, stood my old friend from college, Chris.

"Chris?" I was shocked. I hadn't seen him since graduation, and we hadn't really kept in touch, but I knew him instantly. "What are you doing here?"

"I could ask you the same thing! All roads lead to Rome for us Catholics, don't they?" he joked back.

I let the two people right in front of Chris go ahead of me in the line so I could stand next to him, and for the next fifteen minutes or so, we quickly (and quietly) caught up. He told me he was entering a religious community and was on a trip to Rome with his family, on a sort of "farewell, as you're off to the monastery" trip. I told him I was a teacher and had brought students for a summer pilgrimage. We reminisced about our college days, swapped a few stories about old friends, and then it was my turn to go to Confession.

I gave Chris a quick hug and told him I was so happy we bumped into each other, in St. Peter's no less.

"You know, I almost didn't come over to this part of the basilica," he whispered as we said goodbye. "But I just felt this nudge to come get in the line. Guess you can't ever go wrong getting in a Confession line, can you?"

"No, you really can't go wrong getting in the Confession line," I quipped back. Both Chris and I had hesitated, then listened to the nudge. And from our getting in line came a wonderful reunion with an old friend, followed by being reconciled with the Lord.

I share that story not because I want to convince you to go to Confession so you, too, might reunite with long-lost friends, of course, but because of what Chris said that afternoon: *You can't ever go wrong getting in the Confession line.* It rings true, whether you're on a pilgrimage to Rome or some other iconic holy site, or at your home parish on a Saturday afternoon during the designated Confession time an hour before the Saturday evening Mass. Getting in line is a big step toward the sacrament itself, and we certainly can't go wrong there.

While some of us, sometimes, receive the Sacrament of Reconciliation during spiritual direction in a priest's office or some other place that is not a confessional, most of us will get in line and enter the holy place of a confessional. Whether we are kneeling down behind the screen or sitting across from the priest face-to-face, it is in the confessional that we are able to confess our sins, open our hearts, and graciously receive God's abundant mercy. It's there that we come face-to-face with the love of a Father who desperately wants to heal his children. It's there where we are able to draw close to Jesus, the only begotten Son of that Father, whose death has redeemed us. And it is there, in the confessional, that we are swept up by the Holy Spirit, our vulnerable hearts touched by the words of absolution spoken with gentleness and reverence by the Church's priest.

The Sacrament of Reconciliation is celebrated and its graces are made available to us through a ritual structure, which is known as the Order of Penance. The word *penance* here refers to an outward expression of repenting, or turning back to God. It is not something we do to earn God's grace or forgiveness. Also, in the world of Catholic liturgical celebrations, an *order* is a specific ordering of ritual actions and words into a unified act of worship or what is commonly known as *liturgy*. So, there's an order to the way we go to Confession, and it doesn't begin until we step into the confessional and the priest begins the celebration. He greets us and perhaps offers a word from the scriptures or prays that we may make a good Confession. But our personal preparation for the sacrament must begin before we walk into what Pope Francis had often described as a hospital of mercy, not a courtroom of judgment—the confessional. In the same kind of way we'd have blood work done before a medical appointment, we are expected to do some work in preparation for receiving Reconciliation. Of course, we sometimes delay and struggle with preparing for what to say in Confession. It isn't easy to run the tape back of our sins. It's uncomfortable to run through the Ten Commandments, ticking off the ones we've broken one by one, creating almost a perverted Christmas list we're going to hand to Santa. Instead of gifts I want, here are all the horrible things I've done that prove I'm worthy of no gifts, ever again!

If we think of God like he's Santa Claus, or some genie we coax out of a magic lamp, then yes, getting in the Confession line or examining our consciences can be very challenging. No one wants to go talk to Santa if we know we're on the naughty list. No one wants to call upon the genie if we think he's going to find a loophole to fulfill, or not fulfill, our wishes. No one wants to go to the judge when we know we're guilty and will be sentenced for our crimes.

So maybe the first step to getting into that Confession waiting line, and the most important, is to remember that God is a loving Father, our Savior, and our constant Friend. God longs for us to be there, in the confessional. God wants to see us, love us, forgive and free us, even—and maybe most especially—when we have sinned and are broken and vulnerable. Confession is not about what God wants us to do, but about what God wants to do for us.

For many of us, this is a huge stumbling block. We have a hard time believing we are lovable, that we are wanted by the Lord, and that we are seen, known, and loved, even when we have sinned. To know the love of God, to receive his love and return his love, requires vulnerability, and that is scary, particularly for those of us who haven't been loved as we ought to have been by those closest to us or who have been often and repeatedly let down by those who should love us most.

God's love is perfect. It is abundant. It is complete. God's love is personal and particular, yet vast and sweeping, all at once. God is longing for us to receive his love and rest in it. So, go ahead, get in line.

Learning from Scripture

Get Up

The story of the Prodigal Son, which we encourage you to read, is found in the Gospel of Luke, chapter 15, verses 11–32. It is so familiar that it almost seems too on-the-nose to put it in a book on the Sacrament of Reconciliation. But precisely because of its familiarity, we think it's really helpful to reflect on it.

You likely know how the story goes: A wealthy man has two sons, and the younger son, the baby of the family, asks for his inheritance early. He goes to his father and essentially tells him that he is worth more dead to him than alive, which is such an epic insult that it's a miracle the father doesn't laugh in his son's face and send him on his way. But precisely the opposite happens. The wealthy father gives his son what he asked for, and with his newfound wealth and freedom, a few days later the young son takes off. He is the one we know as the *prodigal*, which, as you can likely work out, means something akin to wasteful or squandering.

That the younger son set off "after a few days" is an important detail in the story that is often glossed over. Basically, the son goes to his dad on a Monday, takes the week to count his money, and then bails by the weekend, which means the father likely spends those days watching his son make plans to go off, probably to squander the money and ruin his life. This raises the first of many essential questions: Why doesn't the father step in? Why does he give his youngest son the money in the first place? Simply: freedom.

The father in this story, and our Father in heaven, will not impose his will. He invites. He encourages. He draws close. But he doesn't force. We, just like that younger son, have immense freedom. We can choose to do good or bad, and the Father lets us. We can head off in the wrong direction and are allowed to do so because of God's unfathomable love. I'm sure part of the father's heart in Luke's story is broken. But part of him probably also knows he's raised his son well and hopes that he has taught his son enough virtue that he won't totally fall prey to sin and darkness.

The story of the reckless, squandering son doesn't give us much detail about how he spends all of what was to be his inheritance, but we do learn that his life is what some translations call "loose living." He has a good time, carefree and with no responsibility. But then he is broke and tending pigs just to stay alive.

Sin can be so alluring. It can seem great, feel good, appear freeing, with just us making our own choices, when and how and because we want to make those choices. But eventually sin will always leave us broken. It will always leave us far from the comfort and certain love of our loving Father.

In his empty brokenness, while slopping pigs and longing to eat trash to try to fill his belly, the younger son wallows. You can almost picture it—and smell it. Sitting in the mud, hungry and alone, he probably reminisced about the good ole days, with his deep pockets and his good time. And as his mind wanders back to when he had enough on his own, there's a clear moment remembering when he had enough, but was not alone.

Luke 15:17 describes the young man as "coming to his senses" and remembering his old home—most specifically, his father. In his mind, as his tummy grumbles and the foul smells overtake him, we can imagine him remembering that back home, under the care and leadership of his father, is a thriving business, servants, and probably plenty of work to be had. The servants have plenty to eat, when they work, so why couldn't he try to do that too?

He resolves to return home to his father. But not as a son. He knows he has messed up. He is totally aware of his faults and failings. This is a broken man, in the mud, with the pigs, far from home, and completely alone. He is under no assumptions that anyone back home would ever want to see him again, much less welcome him back. His father, probably least of all. But as he hatches his plan, he convinces himself that his father could maybe hire him. His father could take pity on him, as anyone would pity a hungry man. His father won't forgive him, but would maybe not totally cast him out if he agreed to earn his keep.

The squandering son, lost and wandering and alone, deeply believes he isn't worthy to be in the family. But he can work for them. He can earn a wage. He can't be loved, but he can have a place to live and work and eat. And so, as we read in Luke 15:20, "he got up and went back to his father."

He got up. Even in the lowest moment of his life, he does not remain in the muck and mud and stench. He gets up. The prodigal son starts to go home. He knows he needs to at least return to where it all began and seek something from his father.

How often have we been in this same position? We can picture it so easily, because we're familiar with the muck and mud of sin. We've fallen and failed, in big and small ways, and in our lowest moments as we are covered in the smelly reality of our sinful ways, we can either wallow or we can get up. The prodigal son shows us the way.

The Father Is Waiting

On his way home, the prodigal son in Luke's story rehearses his speech. We can almost see him walking along that path, traveling for miles, day and night, dirty and hungry. He says it over and over, getting the phrasing just right. "Father, I have sinned . . . against heaven and against you." He's really owning his mistake. He isn't leaving anything to chance. This is the moment to admit his faults, claim his failings, and ask for a bunk in the barn. "I no longer deserve to be called your son." He has even doled out his own punishment. He's trying to make this as easy as possible on the father he is convinced will be prepared to punish him without mercy.

Luke 15 lays out the son's speech. We hear it being rehearsed on the journey home, and within three verses we will hear it again when the son actually says it to his father. It's important that we know the son believes he is unworthy of forgiveness. He has allowed his sin and his shame to consume him, and he thus condemns himself before he even sees his father's face again.

Luke 15:20 tells us the resolve of the son, to get up and go home. And then it also shows us the resolve of the father. "While he was still a long way off, his father caught sight of him, and was filled with compassion." The son is still a long way off, not knocking at the door. He didn't send a message ahead telling the family to expect him. We can even imagine the son trying to sneak into town unnoticed. His father, and his family, seem to have been well-off, perhaps even quite rich, with a good amount of prestige, and would've been known in the town. Maybe the son wouldn't have wanted to bring more shame to his family and so didn't want to make a scene by his returning. But while he is still a long way off, his dad sees him. We have learned something of both the father and the son in just one simple verse from Luke's gospel: The son got up, and the father was watching, and waiting, for his boy.

There is, of course, great significance to the father waiting for his son. We can ponder just how long he had stood at that window, waiting for the maybe-never-to-come return of a child who'd forged his own path. We can consider the sadness in his heart, knowing his son is far away, and he doesn't know what's become of him. Did his son spend his money wisely and double the investment? Did he lose it all and now is he suffering through this famine? The not knowing when, or if, he'd return and what has come of him must have plagued the father.

When he sees him, the father is filled with compassion, and all he can think of is getting to him as quickly as possible. This wealthy, landowning man, with servants that he could've easily ordered to go bring his son into the house, runs to his son. He hikes up his robes and bolts out of the house, down the path, probably in full view of the people who worked for him and people of the town. He embraces his son. He doesn't hesitate. He doesn't hem and haw about the propriety of a powerful man running like a madman to hug his child. He just goes to his son and pulls him close. His lost and hurting child has gotten up to return to him.

Once Lost and Now Returned

The son was likely shocked by this greeting. He's prepared his speech, he's rehearsed his lines, and he knows exactly what he's going to say to just try to get a low-ranking job so he can get some food. He gets his words out, as quickly as he can, and he owns what he has done. He admits his faults and failings. "I have sinned against heaven and against you," we hear again, this time not practiced alone on a long walk, but spoken to a father who has inexplicably run to greet him. He gives himself a punishment, too: "I no longer deserve to be called your son." The son is completely aware of his sin. He is under no allusions that this is something to be glossed over or forgotten. He is ready to own his mistake.

But his chance for self-pity and flagellation are short-lived. Before he can even finish his request to just work as a hired hand, his father tells his servants to bring a robe and a ring and plan a feast. There will be no chance for self-pity or whining here. The father declares, "This son of mine was dead, and has come to life again; he was lost, and has been found."

The celebration begins. Here is the lost, wandering child of a wealthy and powerful man, welcomed home. His absence has been felt. His bad choices have not been ignored. Everyone—the father, the older brother, the servants in the household, likely the whole town—knew this boy had been gone. But his sin did not define this moment. His getting up and returning did. His father's compassionate welcome did. This moment of forgiveness and reconciliation: That was the focus.

The lost son, who had wandered far and sinned much, is the most relatable figure in this parable. Because each of us, in various moments of our lives, have wandered and sinned. We have been lost. We have drifted off the course, choosing ourselves over the Lord, making our wants, desires, needs, and plans the priority. We have fallen, failed, and found ourselves in the mud.

But when we are in that mud, as we hopefully think back to the times when we were not, do we get up? Do we come to our senses and try to return to the home of our Father? Because now we know what is waiting for us at home. Now we know that our Father waits and watches for us. He sees us from a long way off and is filled with compassion.

The son defined himself entirely by his sin. He saw nothing but his wandering mistakes and moments of failure. He wallowed in the wrongs, until he came to his senses and thought that, at the very least, he could earn a small wage and be around the father and his home. He never imagined that his father, wealthy and powerful, would not define him by this colossal error and failure. While the son was finding his identity in his sinfulness, his father still held him close and restored his identity as his beloved son.

This is what happens in Confession. This is why we must come to our senses, get up, and go get in line. Because if we do not—if instead we stay in the mud and merely rehearse a self-condemning speech—then we lose ourselves. Our identity becomes "I am a sinner," but the Father looks at us and says, "You are my beloved child," and pours out tender mercies. Our Father in heaven is watching and waiting, moved with compassion, and he pulls us into his loving arms. We have only to go to him.

Examining and Preparing

Sin is a funny thing. It oddly needles its way into our lives, weasels its way into our hearts, and rests there. One tiny sin becomes a bigger one, a quick mess-up cascades into something larger, and before we know it, we are far from home, starving and alone.

Going and getting in line for Confession, in whatever fashion or form that takes, is an intentional choice to return home. It is us coming to our senses like the lost son. Then we need to contemplate what led us far from home in the first place. And we need to think about and practice what we want to say to our heavenly Father as we return to him.

We don't do this simply to wallow or feel awful. We don't do this because we want to feel bad about ourselves. We do this so we are ready to face our Father. We do this so we know, clearly, what has led us far from him. And we do this so we can be truly honest in naming our error, our sin. Only then will we be free to welcome the grace of forgiveness and the gift of being reconciled with God and with one another.

Notice that the prodigal son speaks first when he meets his father as he returns home. His father has embraced him, and the son quickly recounts his wrongs. The father doesn't ignore what his son is saying. He just greets his son's admission with words of compassion and care. Just so, we examine our consciences so that we can stand before our Father in heaven and recount what we have done with humility and integrity. We recall what has pulled us away from God and other people in the first place, and we long to be assured, "That is not who you are anymore."

Of course, it's entirely possible you do this all the time. Maybe you're the most regular of Confession-goers, with a standing appointment and a place in line. You know how to examine your conscience and, in fact, have a great method for doing so. We also know it's possible that you haven't been to Confession in a very long time for any number of reasons. Life is busy. Time is short. You're perhaps nervous or scared because it has been so long. Maybe you never found it particularly helpful. Whatever has kept you far from the confessional, whether seemingly accidental or on purpose, it's okay that it's maybe been a while. It's likely that most of you are somewhere in between—not opposed or uncomfortable with Confession, but it's just hard to make it a priority. Going to Confession isn't all that high on the priority list. Jesus knows I love him, so why do I need to go sit in a room and talk about all the ways I haven't loved him back?

Wherever you fall on the spectrum of Confession attendance, the room of mercy is waiting for you. The Father is waiting and watching for you. Will you return? Will you come to your senses and go get in line? Will you run back to the Father, as he is running to you?

Thinking and Growing as Parents

Work through the following questions by yourself, and then use them to spark deeper conversation with your spouse, another important adult in your child's life, or the child you are helping to prepare for First Reconciliation.

1. What does going to Confession mean to you? How has it made you feel in the past?

2. When was the last time you went to Confession? How was that for you?

3. If it's been a long time since you've gone to Confession, what has kept you away?

4. When was the last time you told someone you were sorry and asked to be forgiven? When have you been the lost son?

5. When have you been on the receiving end of an apology? What was it like to be in the role of the father in the parable of the prodigal son and to receive someone with compassion?

Growing Together as Parents and Children

We hope the following material will help you have a meaningful conversation with a child preparing to go to Confession, whether for the first time or later on. The sample script offered is meant to be used loosely. Add to it or take away whatever is helpful for you, in the moment, in your particular circumstances. Think of this section as a "choose your own adventure" portion of the book. You can adapt things to use in one-on-one settings, in a school or religious-education program, or with a small group of parents and children learning and growing together.

Confession can seem like an intimidating and scary thing. Go into a room, name your sins to a person, and then walk out again! That's scary for an adult, so is seems likely that it will be scary for a child also. We assumed this would be the case with our daughter Rose, who was seven years old and in second grade when she first received the Sacrament of Reconciliation by making her first Confession. As it turned out, Rose was not as scared as she was overwhelmed by the expectation of reflecting on her life and trying to work out how and why she may have sinned. Her biggest question was, "Where do I even begin?"

In the earliest days of talking about First Reconciliation, the first thing to bring up is not necessarily the "how to do it" or even what to say. The first thing to talk about is that we need to prepare our minds and probe our hearts, slowly and intentionally, by examining our consciences so we know where to begin when we make our way home to the Lord.

Sample Script

Read the Prodigal Son parable (Luke 15:11–32) together, then talk about these questions:

1. How do you think the father felt when his son asked to take the money? *Why?*

2. How would you feel if someone told you they didn't want to be around you anymore and just wanted to do their own thing?

Sin is when we "do our own thing" and leave God, the Father, behind. And God misses us when we're gone. In the Bible story, when the younger son leaves, and after he's had all his fun and spent all his money, what happens to him? How do you think he felt when he was alone and working with the pigs? What do you think made him get up from the mud and go back home?

The lost son is lost! He realizes the bad choices and mistakes he has made, and so what does he do? He gets up! He decides to go home. Do you think he was nervous? How do you think he worked up the courage to go home? What do you think he was thinking about when he was walking home? How do you think he was getting ready to say, "I'm sorry," to his father?

The lost son had to think about everything that had happened. He had to examine his mind and his heart and think about the bad choices, his mistakes, and then have the strength to go admit what he had done was wrong. That takes courage! Now let's practice examining your mind and heart (or "our minds and hearts" *if you want to model for your child how this can be done easily*).

1. When have you been nervous or scared and needed courage?

2. Is there anything you need to say sorry for to the Lord?

3. What mistakes do you know you have made? Can you talk about a time you did something that you knew was wrong?

4. How would you like to take up the responsibility of thinking about those mistakes and get ready to ask forgiveness for them?

In our Bible story, as the lost son gets closer to home, his father sees him because he has been waiting for his child to come home! Why do you think that is? Why do you think the father was waiting for his child at the window? How do you think the father felt when he saw his son?

Once the father sees his son coming toward their home, he runs out to meet his child—runs, at full speed. He must've looked silly! But still, he ran to his son, and nothing would stop him from hugging his child and holding him close. How do you think that made the son feel?

When you go to Confession, you are a lot like the lost son from this story. And just like the lost son, you have to think about what wrong things you've done and prepare to tell our Father that you are sorry. When you examine your conscience (that part of you deep inside that tells you what is right and what is wrong) slowly and prayerfully, it's like you are walking home, just like the lost son who was far away. But who is waiting for you at the end of that long walk? God, our heavenly Father! He's watching and waiting for you to offer you forgiveness and make sure you know just how much he loves you.

Praying as a Family

Wrap up your conversation in prayer. You might pray spontaneously by saying aloud to God whatever is on your heart and encourage your child or the children with you to do the same. Or pray the simple prayer we offer here. Or pray in both ways!

> Heavenly Father, we have sometimes been far from you,
> but we want to come home. We want to be held by you.
> Help us to have courage and strength to get up
> and come meet you in Confession,
> so that we may know your love and mercy anew.
> In the name of Jesus, we pray.
> Amen.

2.

Bless Me, Father

Joining Our Stories to the Church's Story

Tommy: What Could Go Wrong?

Just after Rose turned two, we set out on a little family getaway to Houston, Texas, with some friends. Minutes before leaving, I got a text from my friend David. "There's a community pool within walking distance of the rental house! Bring your swimsuits!" Excitedly, I ran back into the house, grabbed my swim trunks, Katie ordered Rose a new swimsuit for pickup at Target, and we were off for the vacation.

Rose couldn't yet swim, so she'd cling to me as we walked up and down the pool, running her little hands through the cool water and giggling as she splashed it. We were hooked, having the absolute best time. "She's totally gonna be a water bug," I told Katie, confident that I had a burgeoning Olympic swimmer on my hands.

Fast-forward a couple of years, and we finally signed Rose up for swim lessons. Plenty of pool sessions had included Rose clinging to me like a panda that had found the perfect bamboo tree, and she was too tall and gangly to keep that up. It was time for her to swim on her own, and I was confident she'd be good at it.

We arrived at the pool on the first day, and I sent Rose to go stand with the six other kids on the side of the pool while I went to sit with the other parents on a bench by the wall. "Dad, don't leave me!" she instantly whined.

"You'll be fine, bud. I'm right over here." I said back. I knew if I got in the pool, she'd never let me out, and I wanted her to at least try one time without me. But you likely know where this is going . . . I got in

15

the pool about ten minutes later, hoping to prevent a meltdown and a total waste of the class.

The first couple of sessions went fine. Rose learned how to dunk her face in the water, she learned how to kick her feet as she held onto the wall of the pool, and she became a bubble-blowing pro within minutes. But every time the instructor or I would lead her out into the water and then try to let go of her hands, Rose would panic, freeze, wildly flail her arms and legs, and scream. She was gripped with fear the second we'd let go. And when it came to getting her to jump in the water—forget it.

By the end of the week, even with all the lessons, Rose wouldn't let me or the instructor let go of her hands, and she certainly wouldn't jump in. She had been excited for the lessons at first—she'd always had a blast in pools before—and she had followed the instructions perfectly. But the second she'd step to the edge of the pool, a paralyzing terror would take over. She'd close her eyes, count to three, and then still be standing on dry ground. And over and over again, she'd just say, "What if I don't come up?"

She was scared, and, simply put, she had no trust in any of it. She didn't trust the water to hold her up, she didn't trust her legs to bring her back to the surface, she didn't trust that either the instructor or I would help her. She'd never done this before, and every time, she'd be on the brink of a full-blown panic attack as she tried to psyche herself up to jump in the pool. Gone were the days of a two-year-old happily clinging to me as we walked around the community pool with our friends on vacation. Now we had a little girl slowly becoming terrified of the water. And even as I tread water right in front of her, reassuring her that she would be safe, she'd freeze and not jump in.

When the week of lessons ended, Rose got a participation certificate, and Katie and I were stumped. Technically, she didn't know how to swim, it felt as if she was further away from the skill after the lessons, and we were fairly sure we'd done more harm than good in sending her to the class.

"What if you took her somewhere on y'alls own? Just the two of you?" Katie asked me one evening. "University Pool has three-dollar free swim, and you and she could just go practice."

"She won't do it, babe. She's too scared."

"You could just try, maybe?"

So that weekend, early one morning, I woke Rose up, we got our swim gear, and we headed to the pool. On that early summer Saturday, we had the place to ourselves. So into the pool I jumped, immediately turned to face her on the edge of the pool, and commanded her to jump.

"I'll just walk down the stairs, Daddy," she insisted.

"No, Rose. Jump." And I started to lay it on pretty thick. "Daddy is right here. I will catch you. You won't sink. You won't drown. You won't get hurt."

"But what if I do?"

"You won't, Rose. I am right here."

"But what if you swim away?"

"I'm going to stay right here and wait for you."

"But what if . . ."

"Just trust me, Rose! *Jump.*"

Then like a movie scene unfolding in slow motion, her little feet left the still sunbaked and scorched hot concrete, and she launched herself into the water. A huge splash erupted from the water as she crashed into me. She opened her eyes as she wrapped her arms around my neck and shouted, "I did it! And you caught me!"

Katie: What Could Go Right?

Early in his pontificate, Pope Francis offered striking remarks on the Sacrament of Reconciliation to a group of priests and seminarians. "Confession is not a court of condemnation, but an experience of forgiveness and mercy" (Course on the Internal Forum in Rome, March 28, 2014).

In those first few months of leading the Church, the Holy Father wanted us to think differently about Reconciliation, ensuring that we didn't consider going to Confession to be a chore or a place where we'd ultimately be condemned. He wanted to make clear that the only unknown in the confessional is how much mercy will be bestowed, not if it will be given freely. Again and again, he emphasized this point, as have many popes and saints and theologians over the years.

Confession is medicinal. The Sacrament of Reconciliation, from the moment we begin with the Sign of the Cross to the moment we say, "Amen," on the way out the door, is a chance to encounter abundant and perfect mercy. And mercy heals. Yet, at times, we hesitate. We hem and haw our way through the Confession line, or delay going, insisting it's not all that important. Sometimes we psyche ourselves out because we worry about what we'll find inside.

When we talked to Rose about her hesitation to jump into the pool, at first she'd simply say, "I just don't want to." And sometimes, that's a perfectly fine answer. But in this case, we could tell there was something significant holding her back. Her father was in the pool, along with a swim instructor. She was completely and totally safe. In fact, safer conditions couldn't be found, because often she'd insist on wearing arm floaties during the lessons. So, she had a parent, an instructor, and a flotation device. But she also had a whole lot of fear. Jumping in, just simply starting the swimming, was nearly impossible, because she didn't know what *could* happen. The unknown loomed.

After lessons one day, she peppered me with a string of questions: *What if the water is cold? What if Dad gets distracted and doesn't see me jump? What if a floatie falls off? What if I jump wrong and hit my head? What if I sink? What if the other kids make fun of me? What if my bathing suit slips down? What if I get water in my nose? What if my hair gets all chlorine-colored?*

She ran through the tape of all the worst-case scenarios, not knowing if any of them would come to pass. All she could consider was what *could* go wrong. And so, thanks to some tactics learned in therapy, I flipped the script, asking her, "What could maybe go right?"

"Nothing," she whined.

"Or maybe all of it?" I quipped back.

And then my young daughter sat in silence, now picturing water that wasn't too cold, a focused and attentive parent, floaties remaining on her arms, and an elegant dive into a pool that she no longer feared.

Maybe this is the same reason we've stayed far from the confessional. We haven't been in a long time, or the last time we went it wasn't so great, or we think that all the things that could go wrong will go wrong while we sit in a tiny little room and bare our souls.

Father could be unkind or distracted. Confessing sins could dredge up trauma and wounds. Someone will overhear what I say and judge me forever. I won't feel any better when I finish, so why even make the effort? What if it hurts more than it helps? What if the penance is really difficult? What if I hate it? What if I'm judged for needing to go to Confession at all? What if I don't remember the Act of Contrition? What if my mind blanks when I walk in there and I have nothing to say? The what-ifs are long, and those potentially bad experiences loom large.

But what if it all went right? What if, in stepping into the confessional and simply beginning with the words "Bless me Father, for I have sinned . . ." we are reaching out, crying out, for an abundant, perfect, healing love that can only be found when we reconcile with the Lord? And then we will find our Father is waiting for us, with outstretched arms, ready to catch us as we dive into this ocean of mercy.

Learning from Scripture

At the beginning of Luke chapter 8, Jesus tells two parables in rapid-fire succession: the parable of the sower and the parable of the lamp (the inspiration behind the elementary-school favorite song, "This Little Light of Mine"). In these stories, Jesus teaches about what it means to give back to the Lord what he has given to us. At the conclusion of Luke 8, we meet two people, a synagogue official named Jairus and a sickly woman whose name we don't know. This powerful man and this hurting woman, who seemingly have little in common, are a snapshot of each of us as we enter the confessional.

Jesus is making his way through a town where crowds of people have been waiting for him. We can reasonably assume that stories of his casting out demons from a possessed man have spread, as have other tales about this powerful preacher and healer. In this crowd is Jairus, a synagogue official, and we immediately know Jairus is desperate. Jairus falls to Jesus's feet and begs him to come to his home, because there his only child, his beloved twelve-year-old daughter, is sick and dying.

Terrified and heartbroken and so very desperate for healing, a man with power and authority in a place of worship humbles himself before Jesus and asks for his help. He doesn't gesture Jesus off to the side of the road, away from the curious eyes and ears of the huge crowd. He doesn't send word early that he wants to meet with Jesus. No, Jairus cries out for help publicly and doesn't fear whatever reputational harm this might bring him. He is in need of healing for his daughter. In a lot of ways, he may be even in need of healing for himself.

He's got a child on the brink of death. This is ripping him apart, breaking his heart, causing stress and anxiety and fear that are likely keeping him up, night after night. Begging Jesus to come heal his daughter is his last hope. And with that small sliver of hope in his heart, he steps up to Jesus and names his desire for something to be made right again. For twelve years, he has delighted in his daughter, and now she is sick—they both need Jesus.

Luke tells us that Jesus is moved, so he begins to make his way with Jairus to his home, and the crowds gather around him. You can almost hear their shouts; feel the throng of people pressing against one another, smooshed together to try to catch a glimpse of Jesus; hear what he's going to say to Jairus; or see if he can do anything about the dying little girl.

It's in that crowd—maybe on the edge of it at first, but eventually right in the middle—that we meet the second person at the center of this story. She is a woman whose past twelve years have been very different from Jairus's. She's been hemorrhaging, and in her pursuit of a cure and better health, she's gone to every doctor she can find. Every attempt to be healed of her affliction has failed. She is broke, with no money, no livelihood, no sustainable life. No one can help her. No one can touch her. No one can welcome her or offer her comfort, because she is considered unclean.

Mosaic law specifically would have stipulated that she could not present herself at the Temple, she could not be married, and she could not prepare food for others. She is isolated, alone, and broken. This unnamed, bleeding woman is desperate and, like Jairus, must hope that maybe this miracle man can do something for her.

While Jairus walked up to Jesus and cast himself at his feet, naming his hope for healing and begging for Jesus to act, this bleeding woman, whose wounds and blood have kept her far from others for so long, hides in the crowd. She doesn't want to be noticed. She doesn't want the attention. She maybe hopes no one will even realize she's there. But this is her one chance to be cleansed and go on to a new, better life, so she pushes through the crowd that's pressing against Jesus.

She glimpses him slowly making his way to the synagogue official's house. Maybe she has heard about the sick little girl, and so in her desperation she pushes on, perhaps hoping Jesus can heal her first. "What if he can only heal one of us a day? What if it doesn't work? What if I'm bleeding like this forever?"

Then there he is, right in front of her, and no one seems to realize she's the town outcast, the bleeding woman probably pitied and feared. No one seems to notice she's there, just as she had hoped, and there is Jesus, standing close enough that she can touch him. She doesn't need to grab his tunic or even talk to him. She doesn't need an embrace or a conversation. She just needs the hem of his garment. Surely the one who casts out demons and calms the storm can take care of a bleeding woman who briefly touches the tassel on his cloak, right?

There it is, and suddenly it's in her hand, this little bit of fabric on the cloak of the healer. There is no pause for the impact. There's no waiting for comfort. "Immediately her bleeding stopped," we read in Luke 8:44. From just the very edge of his garment, without even speaking a word, she is healed. It worked. It actually worked! I'm sure she was stunned.

Jairus begged for Jesus to come heal his daughter. The hemorrhaging woman reached out to touch Jesus to be healed of her bleeding. Jesus responds to the desire for healing, whether we are explicit and desperate in our request or fearful and uneasy and hiding on the edge of a crowd.

A Faith That Saves

As soon as the bleeding woman is now the healed woman, Jesus stops walking. "Who touched me?" he queries. No one steps forward, and Peter, with his signature sarcasm, reminds Jesus that they're surrounded by people and everyone is touching him. But Jesus insists this was different. This was a desperate touch, a reaching touch, a wordless request for healing just as desperate as the begging of Jairus who is leading Jesus to his home. "I know that power has gone out from me," Jesus says.

The blood the woman has suffered with as long as Jairus's daughter has been alive is now gone. Standing there, no longer stooped over in pain, the freshly healed woman realizes she can't hide in this crowd any longer. She reached out, so now she steps forward, and for the second time that day, someone falls at the feet of Jesus.

The words likely pour out of her, a cacophony of explaining. I'm sure there are repeated "I'm sorrys" and details as to why she felt the need to touch Jesus in the first place. A woman ignored and alone for so long is now center stage in this dramatic, public moment. She has touched the Lord and been healed, and she announces this to Jesus and everyone else present.

Jesus looks at her with tender compassion. How could he not be moved? Her suffering has been so great, and now he sees her desperate touch deeply rooted in a confident faith that he could make her well.

She hadn't spoken aloud her desire to be healed, but she'd reached out all the same. Stretching her arm out to touch the hem of his garment were words enough. "Daughter, your faith has saved you," Jesus tells her. "Go in peace." He sends her forth, healed and now confident in his love for her.

This bleeding woman wordlessly made known her desire to be made well, and Jesus did not hesitate to meet her need, the deepest desire of her heart. This woman recognized her wound and received his healing. We are like her when we step into the confessional knowing we have been isolated and broken by our sins, carrying a pain we have in many cases inflicted upon ourselves. In Confession, we seek reconciliation. We reach out to the Lord to stop the bleeding. We throw ourselves at his feet and give a profound witness to a deep faith: that we know when we reach out, even just the hem of his garment will cleanse our sins and restore our hearts to him. And it is that deep faith and his abundant mercy that completely heal us.

Little Girl, Arise

As all of this is unfolding, Jairus stands there still waiting for Jesus to hurry to his home. He, too, has a deep desire—for his child to be healed. He longs to see her well again. He knows her suffering, as only a father can know. Then, as he waits, terrible news arrives—Jairus's little girl has died. Luke's gospel doesn't describe Jairus's reaction or response, but he surely crumples under the weight of the instant grief. This isn't supposed to happen. This isn't how it's supposed to be. Children should not get sick and die. Especially not when Jesus is near.

We can imagine that Jesus is deeply moved by Jairus's request and now this sudden shock, and so he quickly tells him, "Do not be afraid; just have faith and she will be saved." The faith of the hemorrhaging woman has just saved her, and this crowd of people saw it and heard talk of it. Now Jesus is telling this desperate and hopeful synagogue official also to have faith. Jesus and his disciples set off with Jairus and, arriving at the house, meet a crowd of weeping and mourning people, heartbroken at a child's death.

Confidently, Jesus says she's just sleeping. She's not too far gone. Healing is possible. He asks Jairus to just have faith, which, at this moment, seems to be in short supply. Either word has not yet spread about the bleeding woman's healing, or there is a sadness deeply rooted in their hearts, because no one can imagine Jesus can do anything about the situation.

"They knew that she was dead" is such a clear, concise, confident description of a group of people who have lost all hope. They knew she was beyond the reach of the Lord. They *knew* it. Nothing and no one could tell them otherwise.

When we are hurt, whether by others or self-inflicted, the wounds over time become so deep, so painful, so heavy to bear, that we know they are there. Even when we aren't thinking about them, or can't actively feel them, the wounds are there. In some cases, we cling to them simply because they are familiar. We don't want to shake them off, cast them out, because at least we know what these wounds feel like. When we are embroiled in sin, repetitive or what may seem casual or accidental, our wounds get deeper and deeper. Sin becomes easier and easier. Death, and detachment from the Lord, becomes comfortable, because it is what we know best.

In some cases, we have been hemorrhaging for years. Perhaps some of us have sat in the mud with the swine, longing to eat their food. At times, our life seems to be over. We feel dead. Sin has drained us, left us empty, and killed us. With the same weeping confidence of the crowd gathered at the home of Jairus, we know the end has come.

But this girl's father begged Jesus for help. The bleeding woman reached out to touch the hem of his garment. The lost son got out of the mud and found his way home. We, too, can get up, begin again, start anew. Because we know who waits for us, with tender mercy and love unending.

Jesus does not fear entering into the room where someone seems dead. Jesus does not pull his hem away from the woman's hand. The Father does not reject his long-lost son. We are met by God's mercy, not rejection or scorn. And in the confessional, all weeping, mourning, heartbroken, lifeless, and ashamed sinners are invited and enabled to come back to life.

Entering the room, with just her parents and Peter, John, and James, Jesus holds the little girl's hand. "Talitha koum," Jesus says. "Child, arise!" This is a bold proclamation announced over a little girl who has been lost to this world. *Instantly*, she is restored to life. Just like the woman's blood was dried up immediately. Just like the prodigal son's father was immediately filled with compassion for his long-lost child.

There is no delay when the Father heals. There is no hesitation when Jesus has loved us back to life.

The evangelist Luke likely didn't witness this moment. But when he was inspired by the Holy Spirit to write this account, so that we can read it centuries later and know of the mercy and power of Jesus's healing touch, he described this little girl's parents as "astounded."

Jairus, clinging to his wife and then rushing to pull his daughter close, likely wept. But these tears were not tears of mourning. These were tears of relief. Tears of rejoicing. Tears at the realization that it worked. He begged Jesus for help, and it worked.

Trust in His Mercy

In the Order of Penance, the priest is encouraged to offer some words of welcome and encouragement to the person who has come to receive the sacrament, whether the penitent is kneeling behind the screen or sitting in front of him. Then together priest and penitent make the Sign of the Cross, and the priest offers a brief prayer asking God to help the penitent know his or her sins and receive God's mercy. This simple opening is intended to help us trust that this is where we ought to be and that we are safe. This is an important little moment because it's meant to bring us comfort, assurance of grace, and trust that we will be met with a compassionate mercy that we truly would not have been able to find anywhere else.

Then we boldly and humbly confess our sins. Many people will begin with the simple phrase "Bless me, Father, for I have sinned" and then share how long it has been since their last Confession. Many Catholics grew up with this and like to continue using this opener, but we don't have to. We can simply talk with the priest, naming our sins and perhaps probing more deeply how certain areas of our life are mired in sin. For others, sharing aloud a list of sins generated by an examination of their consciences is a more helpful way of confessing. No matter the particular way you opt to confess your sins, the priest will help you if you haven't received the sacrament in a long while, or feel lost in any way. Just let him know.

As we name our sins aloud, we fall at the feet of Jesus like Jairus. Like the unnamed woman suffering long with hemorrhages, we reach out to touch his garment. We admit, maybe for the first time in a while, that something is wrong and we need help with it. This courageous honesty is at the heart of the sacrament.

Now, needing help and showing up to get it can be scary, especially if you've had hurtful experiences approaching this sacrament in the past or in any number of possible encounters with the Church. Maybe you've been met by a priest who didn't offer encouragement to trust God's mercy, or one who acted more like judge, jury, and executioner. Maybe it's been a very long time since you've gone to Confession, and at this point, you're wondering what's really the point of going now. Maybe you worry that the priest will be so scandalized by something you want to confess that it's better not to offend or burden him with it. Maybe you just worry you'll mess up the words to the Prayer of the Penitent, often called an Act of Contrition, and he'll judge you for being bad at praying.

Every single reason not to go to Confession is one we deeply feel and cling to. In some ways, we hold on to that reason in the same way we sometimes hold on to our sins—we have grown comfortable not going. We know what it feels like to carry our sins and don't know what it feels like to be free of them. What if we don't like freedom? We can get used to the weight, arms full with what we carry.

The what-could-go-wrongs add up quickly. But what if it all went right? What if you fall at Jesus's feet, and you are brought back to life? What if you reach out, and your long suffering is over? What if you go home, and your Father greets you joyfully? What if you jump in, and you're caught and rejoiced over? What if you learn to trust God's mercy—once again or for the first time? What if it all went right? All of it?

Thinking and Growing as Parents

Work through the following questions by yourself, and then use them to spark deeper conversation with your spouse, another important adult in your child's life, or the child you are helping to prepare for First Reconciliation.

1. Is there anything about the Sacrament of Reconciliation that makes you nervous or scared? What do you think could go wrong?

2. Is there anything about the Sacrament of Reconciliation that you are really excited about? What do you think could go right?

3. Have you been to Confession and it was really fruitful and good? How did that make you feel? What details of the experience were helpful to you? How can you try to have these duplicated?

4. Where else in your life have you or do you need to practice trust? When have you had to jump in or reach out in faith and trust that it won't all collapse around you?

5. Is there something in your life that you have been waiting to bring to the confessional and share with the Lord? Is there a wound you've lived with for many years, or something that seems dead in your life for which you want new life?

Growing Together as Parents and Children

Read Luke 8:40–56, the story of Jairus's daughter and the hemorrhaging woman from your family Bible or maybe a children's Bible if you have one. Then use the short summary and following questions to talk about it.

Sample Script

Jairus's daughter was sick, and he wanted to help her, so he went to Jesus. He knew Jesus could help. He believed Jesus could do something to make his daughter well.

1. Do you believe Jesus can heal? What makes you think so or not think so?

2. Have you ever thought about how much Jesus loves you and wants to heal you? What do you think about that? How does that make you feel?

3. Jairus was brave in asking Jesus for help. He threw himself at Jesus's feet and begged him for help. He didn't hold anything back. When have you been brave? When have you asked for help?

4. The hemorrhaging woman had been sick for twelve years. She was hurting, alone and lonely, and had no money. This woman was suffering a lot. She was in pain for twelve long years. Is that longer than you've been alive? What do you think about that? How would you feel about being sick for twelve years?

Just like Jairus, the woman in the Bible story was brave. She reached out to touch Jesus's garment, because she believed that he could do something to help her. She believed he could heal her. Sin hurts us. When we sin, we are wounded, and we need help. We need to ask Jesus for help and reach out to him for healing. What are you excited about for Confession? Is there anything that scares you? Are you nervous at all? How can you be brave?

Going to Confession is like walking up to Jesus, as Jairus did, and asking for help. It's like reaching out to touch the hem of his garment, as the woman in the story did, and hoping for healing. When you go to Confession, you are being brave and reaching out in faith. You are admitting your sin, saying you need help and healing, and then bravely receiving it from the Lord. Do you believe that our heavenly Father will forgive your sins? Do you trust that you will receive mercy?

Praying as a Family

Wrap up your conversation in prayer. You might pray spontaneously by saying aloud to God whatever is on your heart and encourage your child or the children with you to do the same. Or pray the simple prayer we offer here. Or pray in both ways!

> Father, help us to reach out to you in faith,
> knowing you can heal us. Show us your mercy and love,
> and draw us close to you. Help us touch the hem of your garment
> and receive new life.
> In the name of Jesus, we pray.
> Amen.

3

All That We've Done

Joining Our Stories to the Church's Story

Katie: A Foolproof Plan

We had a cat when I was growing up. Her name was Missy, and she was half stray, half family pet, who came and went as she pleased. We also had a dog, Belle, who sat in the corner of the kitchen and ignored all of us the majority of the time. I wanted a pet of my own, a fluffy companion who would curl up at my feet while I read in my room, who would follow me around the house and not regard me with contempt or ignore me altogether. Mom and Dad said no, we didn't need another living thing in the house. Despite my consistent pleading, the answer remained no for years.

Junior year of high school arrived, and the answer was still no, and the desire for another pet had largely left my mind. Until one day, while sitting in Spanish III, my classmate Joey casually mentioned that his family's cat just had kittens. His mom didn't want to keep them, and they didn't know what to do.

"How many kittens?" I asked.

"Do you want one?"

"Maybe . . ." and I let an idea simmer in my mind. "I think I could take one," I told Joey, and he quickly offered to give me one, after school that very day.

A plan was hatched. I texted my mom (from the bathroom during lunch, on the cell phone that was supposed to be off during the day at school) that Joey would bring me home after school that day, and as soon as the last bell rang, off to Joey's house we went to pick up one of the kittens. In my mind, the plan was foolproof.

I'd bring the kitten home, and in the brief half hour that my mom had to go pick up my little sister from her school and bring her home, I'd be home alone. When mom and Laura pulled up, I'd be in the front yard, with the kitten, and claim that I'd found the stray in our yard when Joey dropped me off. It wasn't that unbelievable that there'd be a stray kitten in our neighborhood, and I was certain my parents would let me keep the kitten, since I'd rescued it from our front yard, after all.

Twenty years later, I'm still pretty pleased with my plan, because, for the first few hours; it worked. Mom drove up with Laura, and within about five minutes, the three of us were enamored with the kitten I "found in the yard." My mom said she'd talk to my dad, but sure, for now we could keep the kitten. Then back to work she went.

When Dad got home that evening, he, too, was smitten with the new arrival, but wary of my story. "You found her where in the yard?" he asked.

"Right by the bushes by the road, when you pull into the driveway," I said. Same location I'd told my mom.

"And there weren't any other kittens there?" he pressed.

"Nope. Just her." Dad was skeptical, but he said we could keep her. She'd need to get her shots and eventually be spayed, but for now, she could stay.

Proud of my deception, and convinced that even if they knew I was lying about where the cat came from, they'd let me keep her, I settled into the couch with a book, my new furry friend playing at my feet.

A half hour later, my dad came into the living room. "You know, that kitten doesn't look like a stray. She isn't mangy or scraggly at all."

"Well, maybe she just ran away from home," I replied (my first error of the evening).

"In that case, we should ask around the neighborhood if someone is missing her," was Dad's response.

I quickly agreed, because of course no one would claim the kitten. This was just some silly theatrics I'd agreed to, certain it would convince my dad of the veracity of my claim: This was a stray I'd found in our yard and I was meant to keep her. After a quick dinner, around the block we went, knocking on every door for the next hour, asking neighbors if they'd lost a kitten. She was bundled up inside my jacket, a little furball heat pack that I knew would be sleeping at the foot of my bed that night.

No one claimed the kitten, and no one had even seen a pregnant stray around, including the woman who lived a few houses down that we affectionately called "the cat lady" because she fed some of the stray cats that wandered between the wooded yards and our cul-de-sac neighborhood. So, home we went, me with my new kitten, insanely proud of myself for this foolproof plan.

Once we got inside and I settled on the couch to do my homework for the evening, my mom pressed play on the answering machine in the kitchen. A voice rang out throughout the house. "Mr. and Mrs. Prejean, good evening. This is Joey's mom. We just wanted to say thank you for taking one of our kittens today and giving her a good home. She was our last one we found a home for, and we're so grateful y'all took her. Let us know if you want any of the kitten food or toys we have at the house, and Joey can bring them to Katie at school tomorrow. Thanks again. Bye!" On cue, the kitten that had finally fallen asleep at my feet lifted her little head and meowed.

Katie: It Wasn't About the Cat

I don't remember all that was said the rest of that evening, but I do vividly remember the anger and disappointment of my parents. My mom was exasperated. She couldn't believe I'd so blatantly, purposefully, and manipulatively lied. How could I have stooped so low, just to get a cat? My dad was mortified. I'd agreed to walk around the block and lie, again and again, and ask people if they'd lost a cat, when I knew, entirely and completely, that they hadn't! He wanted to make me walk back around the block and knock on every door again, apologize, and admit that I'd been lying the entire time. My mother only stopped him from issuing that punishment because I had a huge Spanish test the next day and I needed to study. They both agreed I would not be keeping the cat, and before the evening was up, the kitten Joey had given me was safely in the arms of the cat lady down the street.

Something changed that day, I think, within each of us in the family. My parents now doubted me. How could I ever be trusted again? This was both lying and blatantly disrespecting an answer already given, a seemingly unforgivable offense. My little sister was angry with me, mostly because she could tell our mom and dad now viewed me, and maybe even her, with skepticism and disappointment.

And I, deep down, was mortified, mostly with myself. How could I have done something so stupid and so selfish? Would they ever look at me the same way again? Was this an act so low that my mom and dad would only ever think of me as the child who lied about a kitten?

For weeks I withdrew, and not only because I was grounded for quite some time. I went to school, stayed in my bedroom afternoons and evenings, and didn't go anywhere or do anything else. I stopped talking to my parents, ignored my little sister, became snippy with my friends, and became the foul, moody teenager they warn parents about. I stopped playing my violin, I dropped out of speech and debate, and my grades started to slip. I was a mess, all over a stupid cat lie. My foolproof plan had so brilliantly backfired that burns from the blowup stung every day, and I had no one to blame but myself.

I think that was why it hurt so much. I'd let my parents down, and now I felt like they didn't trust me. I'd clearly disappointed my little sister, who certainly didn't revere me, but didn't think I'd so boldly lie to our parents. And I'd done it all knowingly, willingly, and seemingly without hesitation. I'd chosen to do it, and my plan had so spectacularly failed that now I was living with consequences I hadn't anticipated in the least. I had sinned, and I knew it. The sin itself, at the time, seemed like no big deal. But the fallout felt like an earthquake.

After a few weeks of misery and moping, I found myself sitting across from the rector of my school, Fr. Whitney, in the confessional. The quarterly Confession for students had finally arrived on the calendar, and while I generally wasn't a fan of going to Reconciliation in the middle of the school day (purely on the grounds of not wanting to leave class), I made my way to Confession, hoping that maybe I'd feel just a little bit better.

There I sat, listing off sin after sin, finally arriving at the biggest of them all. I admitted to a priest I deeply admired how big of a lie I'd told to my parents, about something so dumb that I felt simultaneously ridiculous and embarrassed as the words fell from my mouth. I was certain he was judging me, *tsk*ing in my direction as his disappointment with me grew. I couldn't stand to look at Father as I told him the story of what was, up to that point, my deepest shame, and I kept my eyes cast downward as I took a deep breath and said, "I think that's it. And I just feel awful."

"Well . . ." he began as I braced myself. While I'd never known Fr. Whitney to be anything but kind and levelheaded, I just knew he was going to scold me for the stupidest sin I'd ever committed. I took a deep breath. "Can I ask you something, Katie?" he gently said.

"Sure . . ." I mumbled.

"It wasn't about the cat, was it?"

Katie: The Truth We Hide

For the next few minutes, Fr. Whitney lovingly talked me through everything, from reasons why any of us sin to the very particular circumstance in which I found myself. His conclusion was simple: We sin because we think it'll make us feel good, and then we convince ourselves of our invincibility because we feel as if we've gotten away with it. In the end, yes, I'd sinned by lying about a cat. But really, I had been prideful, arrogant, and tried to take matters into my own hands, and the sin was rooted there, not just in the dishonesty and deception.

When sin comes crashing down, we often end up feeling lower than we did before sinning in the first place. And then that sin morphs into shame and guilt that eats away at us, and we draw inward, crushed by our failures. We become avoidant, running from the truth and others. We begin to hide from an uncomfortable reality: Whatever we did was an act of selfish, prideful rebellion. When we sin, we rebel against God, others, and even our truest selves, and we feel such shame for that rebellion. We are exposed and vulnerable, like Adam and Eve in the Garden of Eden, because we've done wrong, been caught, and can't stand the thought of being seen in that state.

"Stop beating yourself up," Fr. Whitney chided. "You came to Confession, didn't you? You came here to heal. It wasn't about the cat, Katie. Maybe at first, but not now. Now it's about moving past what you did and saying you'll do better next time." Then he sent me on my way, with a simple penance to apologize to my parents—maybe with a written letter sharing with them all that I'd shared with him—and to say a decade of the Rosary, that very day. Before I left, he made me promise that next time I felt so low, so ashamed, and so far from the love of God, I wouldn't hesitate to go to Confession right away. "It's good that you came," he told me as I stood up to walk out. "You are not the girl who lied about a cat. You're so much more. You are loved."

Learning from Scripture

An interesting thing happens every time I step into the confessional, and maybe it happens for you, too. I can't seem to look up as I name my sins. Whether I'm kneeling behind the screen or sitting in front of the priest, face-to-face, I cast my eyes down. It's as if the weight of my wrongdoing and the shame of my sin forces my eyes down, my eyelids heavy. Even if I'm ready to be vulnerable and speak my sins out loud and ask God for mercy, my gaze and my heart remain cast down. I saw this same thing with Rose when she lied about YouTube. She ran to her room and hid. She didn't want me to see her, and she didn't want to see herself. Shame isolates, cuts us off, and drives us off on our own, away from those who could even help us to see the love of the Father we so desperately need.

Like the prodigal son who squandered the family riches and the hemorrhaging woman who was alone in her sickness, the Samaritan woman at Jacob's Well in the Gospel of John (4:4–42) is given no name. But Jesus seems to be waiting for her as she shows up at noon to draw water. He "had to pass through Samaria," not because of a travel schedule, but out of a necessity only he seemed to know. Normally Jews and Samaritans were loath to interact. But Jesus asks the woman for a drink. She refuses—incredulous, she wonders what he could possibly be after.

Samaritan women didn't draw water at noon, when the sun was beating down and the well had baked in the hot sun all morning. They went before dawn and carried giant pots of water back to their homes so they could cook and clean and drink throughout the day. But she was there at midday, long after the crowds of other women had gone.

We can surmise from the story that this woman wanted to make her way through life without drawing attention to the burden of shame she carried with her each day—a shame that, despite maybe her best efforts, was no secret. The woman seemingly was divorced and remarried, with five husbands in her lifetime, and was now with a man not her husband. She would have heard the whispers behind her back and known her neighbors stared and gossiped as she walked by, calling her names; perhaps she was taunted even by children. Going to draw water at midday would have kept her from all that.

The nameless woman in John 4 balks at Jesus's request. How can Jesus ask her for something to drink? Jews did not mix or mingle with men or women of Samaria, and they certainly didn't pour drinks of water for one another at random wells in the desert. But Jesus is undeterred by her skepticism, and without mincing words, he explains that he can offer living water. But this is a woman with a tough disposition. She has no time for silly riddles or cryptic musings of a random Jewish man sitting by the well asking for water, when he doesn't even have a bucket.

Jesus presses on, insisting that water from Jacob's well will not quench the endless thirst that we all bear. He offers water that will give eternal life, a spring of water that will satisfy even the deepest thirst for something everlasting and true.

Without hesitation, the Samaritan woman asks for *that* water. She wants this eternal life. Who wouldn't? She longs for that water which will quench a burning thirst once and for always. She makes it clear to Jesus that she doesn't want to return ever again to that well of ordinary water and harsh reminder of her sin.

Shame kept the Samaritan woman from going to the well with all the other women before the sun came up. Shame keeps our eyes cast downward in the confessional. Shame isolates and hides us. Shame cripples us. Shame drives us to the well in the desert at noon, hoping we won't be seen. Shame sometimes keeps us from going to the confessional at all. At other times, shame keeps something off the list in Confession or out of our conversation there.

This woman's shame isn't about the well, just like my story wasn't about the cat or Rose's about YouTube. It's about what we know sin has done to us. It's about what we know we have done to ourselves when we have sinned.

Everything I Have Done

The Samaritan woman makes clear to Jesus what she wants, and Jesus invites her to admit her shame and then to accept him as the long-awaited Anointed One, the Messiah. By saying yes to the living water and to his true identity, the woman is freed—to leave behind the burden of her water jar and the oppressive midday sun. And then she goes into the village to urge the people there to go out to meet Jesus. She raises the possibility to them that he is the Messiah. Not only is this woman freed of the shame of her sinfulness, but she is freed to testify in such a way that "many of the Samaritans of that town began to believe in him" because of her word.

Jesus's life-giving water is available to us, and his healing is within reach. We don't have to return to the source of our shame again and again. We can be freed from the chains of sin and shame. But we can't drink that water if we have no cup. We can't heal if our mouths are closed and our hands are tied. We won't be freed if we cling to our shame.

Jesus sat at a well, waiting for this woman, not because *he* was thirsty, but because she was. She was thirsty for the truth to be known, that what she had done was not the sum of who she was, nor all she ever would be.

When this woman goes back to her town, the first thing she shares with everyone is "He told me everything I have done!" She doesn't quote Jesus's words about the Spirit or the living water or the hour of worship to come. She tells them that Jesus saw her in her sin, saw her in her shame, and spoke to her still, healed her still, loved her still. She did not feel cast out, judged, or condemned. Instead, she felt known and loved. She felt seen. And *that* is what she can't keep to herself. That is what compels her to rush back to her own people and proclaim the truth that has changed her life.

Jesus never even takes a drink of water at the well. And for all we know, neither does the woman he met there. In fact, she has abandoned her water jar. This incident was not about drawing water from that well. No, this story is about Jesus, our all-loving and merciful God.

What We Have Done

It's one thing to get in line to examine our conscience, and it's another thing to step into the confessional and be greeted with the hope that we will make a good Confession with the help of God's grace. But now comes the hardest part. We have to speak our sins aloud. We have to name what we have done. We've thought about it. We've shown up to say we want mercy. We've come to the doctor's office hoping to be well. But now we have to actually talk to our physician. Now we have to name the aches and pains, the ailments and wounds, most of which are self-inflicted.

The *Catechism of the Catholic Church*'s paragraph 1455 says we must look "squarely at the sins" and "take responsibility for them." We don't do this because we want to hate on ourselves or merely wallow. The prodigal son didn't sit in the mud and just bemoan his bad choices and misfortune. He saw what he had done and was determined to go home to set his life on a new path. What he never expected was his father's forgiveness. When we sit in the mud, hopefully we recognize we can get up and go home to the arms of our loving Father, by way of the merciful Savior, whose Spirit guides us to be open to the Lord's presence in our lives again. We take this responsibility seriously, name what we have done, and let the Lord see us as we truly are.

We long for forgiveness not just because it feels good in the end. In fact, when we name our sins aloud in the confessional, it feels decidedly *not* good. We rightly squirm a bit, knowing we've done these objectively bad and wrong things, and now we are saying that we've done them to another person, sitting right in front of us.

But when we say our sins, clearly and without hemming and hawing around what we have done, then we are *owning* our stumbles and admitting that we have fallen. Importantly, too, we know we are saying those sins not to some random person we found on the street. We're in the confessional with the priest, who welcomes us in place of Christ and engages us with the same loving compassion and call to new life that Jesus offered to the Samaritan woman as he sat by the well. The priest stands in for Jesus, listens to us with the love of the Lord, and gently guides us to a deeper awareness of the mercy of God. After we've honestly confessed, *then* we can stand back up, dust ourselves off, accept the Lord's help and love, and move on. Then we can look squarely at our sins, with the help of the priest who stands in place of the person of Christ, and say confidently, "This is not all that I am."

This is an important point we do not want to shortchange. A fine Confession is one that includes a cursory listing of the Ten Commandments you've broken, perhaps cutting things short with a "For these and all my sins, I'm sorry." Quick, in and out, no fuss no muss. To be fair, sometimes a quick Confession is necessary, so long as we don't hide or purposefully leave out any sins.

But we were not made for merely fine Confessions. We were not made for quick listings of what we've done, so that we don't have to sit or kneel there longer than we want, or to avoid "scandalizing" the priest with the worst moments of our lives. We were made for honest, vulnerable, thorough Confessions that name each sin clearly, as well as the number of times we have committed each sin; and we should aid the priest in giving us a good penance and advice by stating the reasons for the sins. We name the kind and number of our sins to be specific, because this is how we own our transgressions. We did these particular things. We need to name them. We offer insights into the reasons why we did them, not to justify our wrongs, but to give context for what in our lives could be leading us astray or driving us to certain repetitive sins. How can we say that the Lord has told us all we've done, and seen us as we truly are, if we are hiding our sins, or mumbling our way through a boilerplate list of sins generated by an AI chatbot? Vulnerability, honesty, and humility are what we should pray for as we examine our consciences and then name our sins in the confessional.

In the confessional, we stand at the well, sometimes at the hottest part of the day, shrouded in our shame. We *could* be swallowed by the depths of our depravity. Or we can look at that well and see the Lord waiting for us there, with life-giving water bubbling up to cleanse us anew and restore us again.

As we name all that we have done, clearly and without hiding any of it, Jesus reminds us of who we truly are: his beloved.

Seeing Sin Leads to Love

It may seem counterintuitive to list our sins and then love God more. Here are all the ways I haven't loved God and, voila, now I love God more because I've named all my failures. How could that possibly work? Then again, how could death on a Cross be deemed the greatest victory of all time? Christianity is nothing if not a series of contradictions that, in the end, make perfect sense when we dive into the mystery.

When we name the ways we have drifted from the Lord and state our sins in Confession, we are clearly saying that we know what we have done is wrong, and we detest those wrongs and do not want to do them again. We are saying sorry. When we say sorry and reconcile with the one we love that we have hurt, it deepens our love. Our sin has made God absent in our lives. Naming the sins and asking for forgiveness means we want God's presence back, and when an awareness of his presence returns, we can't help but be caught up in his love.

The prodigal son knew he had done wrong and was willing to go home and own up to his faults. He was ready to admit his failings, and he expected admonishment and punishment. He was met with his father's embrace and was welcomed home.

Jairus worried for his daughter and asked for healing. He longed for a miracle, for his child to be saved, and Jesus delivered. Jesus brought her new life.

The hemorrhaging woman, broke and alone and in pain for over a decade, reached out in faith, desperate for something new. She was cleansed and comforted by Jesus himself. Her abundant faith was a profound witness to everyone then and is to us now.

The woman at the well, steeped in shame and thirsty for something true, was seen, known, and loved for the first time. She confronted her sinfulness and was transformed by the gaze and words of Jesus, and then she couldn't keep it to herself. She had to go tell everyone in the town what she had experienced.

When we examine our consciences with humility, ask and reach out for healing, confident in Jesus's power, and then confront our sins head-on in the confessional, we can be certain we will be met by the embrace of the One who knows what we need, knows all that we have done, and loves us still.

Thinking and Growing as Parents

Work through the following questions by yourself, and then use them to spark deeper conversation with your spouse, another important adult in your child's life, or the child you are helping to prepare for First Reconciliation.

1. How did you feel the last time you went to Confession? Did you feel better after you made your Confession? Did you hold something back that you knew you should've confessed?

2. Think back to a "big sin" moment in your life. Have you felt shame and embarrassment because of this sin? Have you confessed it and made amends?

3. Have you ever avoided bringing something up in Confession? Why? What kept you from being honest in the confessional?

4. Is there anything that confuses you about Confession? Is there anything practical you would want to ask the priest about what he thinks, prays about, or has learned over the years of hearing Confessions?

5. If you had to tell someone, "This is why I like going to Confession," what would you say? If you had to explain to someone, "This is what keeps me from going to Confession," what would you say?

Growing Together as Parents and Children

Use the following material to dig into conversation(s) with your child about the words and actions of going to Confession and receiving the Sacrament of Reconciliation.

As the Sacrament of Reconciliation begins, after you've made the Sign of the Cross and Father has asked for grace to pour upon you so that you can make a good Confession, it's time to begin listing what you've done. Quite frankly, that is very difficult sometimes.

When we sat down with Rose to do an examination of conscience right before going to the church for her first Confession, she looked up at us, almost crying, and said, "This is gonna take forever!" We had to swallow our giggles, because how could our precious little seven-year-old have *that* much to confess? But, praise Jesus, she took it very seriously, sitting quietly with the examination of conscience we wrote for her (and that's at the back of this book).

We watched as our little girl read through the list, sometimes subtly nodding or shaking her head as she reflected on each question. When she was done, she asked if she could have a pencil so she could circle the ones she'd need to say. This struck us as a great and practical idea—to literally list out what we've done and take that paper into the confessional. Just be certain to rip it up or burn it when you're done, or at the very least not put your name on it! Rose ripped her paper as we left the church that evening, tossing the tatters into a small wastebasket by the side door. She bounced to the car, still grinning from ear to ear—that paper, and those sins, long gone.

It's important to be specific and clear when we talk about the specificity and clarity we need in the confessional. We aren't naming our sins to try to scandalize the priest or to make ourselves feel bad. We are naming our sins, what we did, how frequently we've done them, and maybe even why we've done them, because it helps us to see how far we have run from the Lord, and it helps the priest give us the best advice to avoid those sins in the future.

Sample Script

Read aloud John 4, the story of Jesus and the woman of Samaria, then together pose and respond to these questions:

1. The Samaritan woman at the well was hiding from everyone in the town and in her life. Why do you think she was hiding?

2. The woman listened to what Jesus had to say, even though she didn't know who he was or what he was up to. She didn't think Jesus should be talking to her, let alone helping her. Have you ever been so ashamed of something that you've hidden? Have you ever worried that Jesus couldn't love or heal you?

3. When Jesus asked the woman at the well to think about what she had done, he did so gently and with kindness. He wasn't harsh or mean. Jesus invited her to think about her life and think about where she had made mistakes. What are some things you need to pray about before you go to Confession? Are there any sins you need to think about and know that you must bring up in the confessional?

When we go to Confession, it's kind of like we are standing at a well, just like this Samaritan woman. And Jesus is waiting for us there. He isn't waiting for us because he wants to scold us or punish us. He's waiting for us because he wants to give us something. What do you think Jesus wants to give you?

In Confession, you need to name your sins. You can't just say, "All my sins, I'm sorry." You can say at the end of your Confession that you are sorry for all your sins, even the ones you've maybe forgotten, but you can't purposefully skip sins that embarrass you. And when we name our sins, Jesus doesn't get mad at us, or yell at us, or tell us that we're bad. Jesus offers us living water, he offers us healing, just like he offered it to the woman at the well, and he shows us that we are loved.

Praying as a Family

Wrap up your conversation in prayer. You might pray spontaneously by saying aloud to God whatever is on your heart and encourage your child or the children with you to do the same. Or pray the simple prayer we offer here. Or pray in both ways!

Heavenly Father,
help us to see clearly all that we've done
that pulls us away from you.
Give us the strength to long for, and receive,
the life-giving mercy you have for us.
In the name of Jesus, we pray.
Amen.

4.

It's Really All Gone?

Joining Our Stories to the Church's Story

Katie: Exploding Slushy

The day of Rose's First Reconciliation, her second-grade class went on a field trip to a Christmas tree farm. As I dropped her off that morning, assuring her I'd meet her out at the farm since parents couldn't ride on the bus, she asked if the school had scheduled the field trip on the same day as First Reconciliation so she and her classmates would have more sins to confess that night. I'm still not sure what she thought was going to happen on that bus ride!

We had a lovely morning at the farm, taking a hay ride, petting donkeys, climbing all over a giant swing set, and eating a picnic lunch among the rows and rows of growing Christmas trees. After a quick stop off at the gift shop, parents checked their children out and headed home at their leisure. Rose climbed into my minivan and promptly dozed off in the backseat, right as I pressed play on an examination of conscience for kids. And so, for about a half hour, I found myself going through the Ten Commandments on the winding state highway from Oberlin to our home in Lake Charles, Louisiana, thinking of all the times I myself had failed and fallen. By the time we stopped at a gas station, I was fairly convinced that I needed to go to Confession that night along with accompanying Rose.

Once inside the station store, Rose asked, "Can I have a slushy, Mom?"

"Sure, bud." Who am I to deny a seven-year-old a frozen treat after a field trip?

"I can fill it up myself," she confidently announced as she grabbed the cup with the iconic domed lid and headed to the machines that were churning their frozen, slurpy goodness.

I wanted a cup of coffee, so I stepped to the side to fill up a foam cup with the hot liquid that would give me energy for the rest of the drive home, and in the brief second I turned my back, I heard Rose screech, "Oh no, it's so cold!" I whipped around, and there Rose stood, her hands, shirt, and the floor covered in bright red slushy.

"It was an accident, I swear!" she quickly sputtered, frozen in place as the slushy drink hardened on her little hands. I set my coffee cup down, took a deep breath, and turned fully toward my petrified daughter while also scanning for napkins or a towel I could quickly grab.

"Mom, I'm so, so sorry!" she kept saying, shaking her head in shame and embarrassment.

"It's okay, Rose, it's okay," I quickly said back as I reached for a pile of tiny brown napkins that would do very little to sop up the mess.

"I didn't mean to! It just exploded when I pulled the lever, I swear," Rose kept saying, insisting she had no idea the slushy would flow out of the spout so quickly.

"I promise it's okay. I guess the exploding slushy decided it didn't need a cup!" I joked, gently wiping off the slushy mess from her hands, now bright red from the cherry flavoring and the cold of the slush mix.

"It's on my shirt, Mom," Rose said, so softly and pitifully, so ashamed of the mess all over her, you'd think she'd thrown slushy on the *Mona Lisa*.

"It's fine, Rose. I promise, it's fine. We can wash it." I continued to wipe her hands, shirt, and then the floor, with at least fifty brown paper napkins wadded together.

In that moment, as Rose stood there, teeth chattering because she was both cold and embarrassed, the red stains setting into her gray school spirit T-shirt, I thought to myself, *No one told me how much wiping there'd be in motherhood . . . noses, bottoms, hands, counters, gas station floors.* As I chuckled to myself, continuing to wipe up, I looked up to see Rose's lip trembling as if she was bracing herself for my ire.

"Rose, what's wrong?" I asked.

"I'm just so sorry. It's everywhere," she whimpered back. "I have to wear this shirt tomorrow," and then she looked down at the large red splotch covering the bottom half of the T-shirt.

I finished wiping up the majority of the mess, the lady behind the counter finally coming over with a mop and shooing us away, insisting she would take care of the rest. I gently led Rose down an aisle, and surrounded by Chex-Mix and candy bars, her tears finally fell. "Rose, it's okay. It's just a shirt."

"It's stained red, Mom!"

"Well, we can wash it. The red will come out."

"But it's *bright* red! And my hands are so cold," and she continued to blubber, a combination of overstimulation from the field trip and her fear about the mess mixing together to form the perfect storm.

"Shirts can be washed. Rub your hands together, and they'll warm up, and we'll go fix a new slushy, bud," I said, as matter-of-fact as I could muster. I pulled her into a hug, the cold red stain on her shirt hitting my jacket and leaving a little residue on the lapel.

"You're not mad?" Rose asked, stunned.

"No, bud. I'm not mad."

I held my daughter for a few seconds, her breath finally slowing down. I knew she felt awful, and I knew she was terrified I was on the brink of disciplining her for making a huge mess, even if it was accidental. But I also knew that the guilt she felt, the embarrassment she was carrying, and her frustration about the stained shirt were truly lesson enough. No one can discipline a heartbroken and ashamed child better than themselves. She was making a mountain out of a molehill, no one was all that mad, and yet she was a total mess.

"I don't have to have a slushy, Mom. I don't deserve it," she said as she leaned into me, tears still quietly streaming down her face.

"Do you want cherry or Coke, or a mix?" I asked as I pushed her back and looked her in the eye. I could see it all in that moment: her shame and embarrassment, the slight pain she still felt from the cold slushy that had been on her hands, and her nerves about making her first Confession later that night.

"Are you sure? That spill was bad, and my shirt is ruined," she quietly whispered. I'm not even sure she knew all that she was feeling, but she was confident she no longer deserved, or would get, a slushy.

"Of course, Rose," and I walked over to the machine, grabbing a fresh cup and lid to fix the frozen treat for my verklempt firstborn.

As I mixed together Coke and cherry slush mix, creating the perfect frozen treat in the cup for the little girl who had just made a huge mess, I explained to her that this was no big deal. I assured her no one was coming to yell or fuss, and the great advancements in stain removal technology would clean up her shirt (I hoped). There was no reason to let this ruin the day. I could handle the mess, and she could still enjoy the sweet treat.

As I handed her the cup, Rose took a deep breath, hesitantly took the first sip, and broke out with the biggest smile. "Best slushy ever!" she immediately declared.

Tommy: Red Dye 40

I got home around four o'clock and knew I was walking right into the eye of a storm. Katie and Rose had been on a field trip all morning, then headed straight to piano lessons that afternoon. Rose needed a scrub down from the dusty farm, Katie probably needed an introverted moment alone, and there was truly no telling what was happening with our youngest, Clare, so I braced myself before I stepped into the house.

We come in and out of our home through the garage, right into the laundry room, which usually holds the remnants of a day. Nap mats from school, dirty socks and shoes that need a refresh, occasionally a pile of groceries or supplies that need to be sorted, and clothes—clean, dirty, and everything in between.

Sitting atop the washer, with a scrub brush and a bottle of stain remover, was Rose's spirit shirt for school, which we had bought at the beginning of the school year. It gets worn every Wednesday, for every field trip, and on any spirit-dress days. When we first decided on Catholic education for our kids, I had to be convinced the expensive uniforms were just part of the deal. And to be honest, they look adorable in their plaid jumpers, though I've never fully agreed with the excessive expense of Catholic school uniforms. Knowing how pricey each item is ($38 plaid jumper, $19 shirt, $5 undershorts, $8 white socks and tights, and that's not even accounting for the monogrammed outerwear required on chilly days), Katie and I have been obsessively diligent about stain treatment, writing McGrady on every tag, and ensuring uniforms don't get lost or piled up in a mountain of laundry week after week. We've impressed upon our girls, probably to the point of annoyance, that we are to take care of these uniforms, not get them too dirty, and never lose them.

But there, sitting on the washer, was this year's school spirit shirt, the only one we have for Rose, covered in red splotches and cleaning solution. The scrub brush had the remnants of red on the bristles, the

stain remover nozzle was dripping onto the washer lid, and as I rounded
the corner, Katie was standing at the sink, washing her hands, red water
flowing down the drain.

"Uh . . . everything okay?" I gently whispered, approaching my
clearly stressed-out wife with caution.

"Slushy explosion. Probably ruined the shirt. Second one this
month," she frustratingly mumbled back. I had entered the hurricane,
it was a category 5, and I'd likely missed the brief quiet part that came
with the eye. We were on the dirty side of the storm now.

"Other than that, how was the day?" I gingerly asked. If I've learned
one thing in almost a decade of marriage, it's that I approach my wife
doing laundry with caution.

"Fine. Field trip was nice. Kids ate Cheetos on the hayride, which
was gross, but other than that, it was fine."

Cheetos on a hayride does sound gross, I thought to myself. "And
what happened here?" I pointed to the shirt on the washer.

Katie turned, leaned against the sink, looked at me with utter exhaustion, and sighed out, in one breath, "We stopped at a gas station. Rose
wanted to get her own slushy, the lever popped somehow, and it exploded
all over her. She was very upset. I didn't yell, but the shirt is ruined and
she has to wear it tomorrow, so I have to wash it somehow, or she's just
always going to have to wear it covered in red stains. She's in the bathtub
now. I told her I needed a minute. She doesn't know I'm in here trying
to save the shirt, because I told her it wasn't that big of a deal because I
didn't want her to be too sad. She was already being really hard on herself.
And I think Clare dumped a bucket of LEGOs out on the floor of the
playroom, so be careful when you walk through. They're everywhere."

"Oh, just that?" I tried to joke back, hoping to get my wife to smile
in the midst of the clearly chaotic afternoon.

"It isn't funny," she quickly retorted.

"A LEGO minefield is kind of funny . . ." I mumbled back, turning
to finally get a good look at the shirt.

There it sat, the giant red stains practically leaping off the over-
priced spirit shirt. "Did you scrub the stain stuff in already?" I asked.

"Of course, I did," Katie snapped back.

Proceed with caution, Tommy, I reminded myself.

"Should we wash it on hot or cold?" I asked, lifting up the shirt,
opening the washer lid to see if there were other things inside.

"I was going to look up to see what to do. I'll probably wash it on hot with some color-safe bleach," Katie said, defeated and disgruntled. "It's gonna be okay, babe," I offered. "It's just a shirt. We can buy another one, if we have to."

"It *isn't* just a shirt, Tom!" she shouted back. Whereas most people use a full name when they're upset with someone (we practiced shouting our children's full names before bestowing them, just for the yellability factor—Rose Elizabeth McGrady just rolls off the tongue when you have to drop the hammer, doesn't it?), my wife shortens my name from Tommy to Tom when there's a battle brewing. "It *isn't* just a shirt, *Tom*" was a warning shot across the bow. And I was woefully unarmed.

"What's it about, then?" I asked, trying to be sincere and curious and not cocky and sarcastic.

"I held it together at the gas station and didn't get mad. She was mad enough at herself!" Katie looked like she was suddenly on the verge of tears. "But it was careless of her, and now the shirt is ruined. I feel bad that I'm frustrated about it, because I know she was frustrated too. I just need to let it go and not accidentally mess up tonight. Forgive and forget, right? It just won't be easy."

"Well, yes. Forgive, babe, but also there is work we now have to do. I get it; that's upsetting. You can be upset. Rose was upset. You held it together for her, so now you can be upset too."

Katie nodded.

"Rose probably still feels bad, and you should tell her you're upset as well, but not mad at her about it. Shoving it down won't help. You won't forgive and definitely won't forget if you do that," I told her.

"You're probably right," my wife sheepishly mumbled.

Mark it down, I thought. *December 18, 2024, my wife told me I was right, over a laundry and forgiveness dispute, no less!* "And babe," I approached her cautiously, to pull her into a hug. "I think we can get the red dye out. I'll take care of it, okay? Let me try. Even if it isn't easy."

Learning from Scripture

Is It That Easy?

As Jesus went about during the three years of his public ministry preaching and teaching, stopping in cities, towns, and small villages, and wandering off into the desert, he seems to have been always surrounded by people. Crowds, both big and small, with both new and familiar people, followed him. Rare was the time he was alone, except for the moments he went off by himself to pray and rest.

He was at home one day, maybe even looking forward to some down time, when the crowds found him, and they did what crowds do: They crowded. Before Jesus and the apostles probably even realized what was happening, dozens were crammed into the house. Jesus was at home, and he was teaching, and no one wanted to miss it. The Gospel of Mark alerts the fire marshal by telling us, "There was no longer room for them, not even around the door," as he describes the crowds that have literally crowded in to catch a glimpse of this captivating preacher in Mark 2:2–12.

Into that crowd, enter the four best friends that anyone could hope to have, carrying their paralyzed companion on a mat. They have heard stories about this preacher, knew maybe some of the miraculous things he's done, and they have a glimmer of hope in their hearts: Could he help their friend?

Hope is a compelling virtue, this belief in something possible, the potential of a new reality right there. Hope compels us to look forward, look upward, look longingly at what could be. These four men are driven by a confident hope that if they're near enough to Jesus, he could act. But they're blocked by the crowds. They can't even access the door, can't hear this preacher's voice, much less see him.

But hope doesn't cast our eyes down in defeat. Hope doesn't let the shame of failure swallow us up. Hope lifts our eyes up. And that's when they see it: a roof—a flat roof, likely thatched with simple branches and reeds easily disassembled. Surely Jesus wouldn't mind? Seemingly without hesitation, they pull the branches away from the timber beams and lower down their paralyzed friend until he's there, right in front of Jesus, the gathered crowds probably stunned by the spectacle.

Mark's gospel is famously thin on details—including settings, dialogue, and emotions of the people in the gospel's stories. It's the shortest of the gospels, with Jesus seemingly always on the move. So, with this story, all we know is this man is paralyzed and four men are doing whatever they have to so they can get him close to Jesus. He sees their faith, their desperation, and their hope. Jesus is aware of what it took for the four men to get their friend close to him and immediately says, "Child, your sins are forgiven."

All we know about this man is that he's paralyzed, and yet the first thing Jesus says to him is not "Get up and walk" (that will come, in time). Jesus doesn't inquire about his inability to walk. He doesn't demand an explanation for why the roof is gone. Rather, Jesus addresses the paralyzed man as "Child," but not with scorn, and then, without hesitation, Jesus forgives the man's sins.

The scribes, reasonably so, are confused, accusing him of blasphemy. Only God can forgive sins, so does this Jesus fellow think he is God? Jesus knows what confusion this might cause. He forgives this man's sins, which are not visible to this crowd as are the man's paralyzed legs, which confine him to the mat he lies on. Jesus leans into the confusion of the crowd. He knows the people don't understand and need something else, something tangible, to see that he has done something remarkable. And he begins to ask the crowd, "Which is easier? To say to the paralytic, 'Your sins are forgiven,' or to say, 'Rise, pick up your mat, and walk'?"

Trick question, Jesus. Both of those things are hard, because both are miraculous moments of healing. But, in this context, the crowd probably thinks it'd be easier to just "magic away" the sins. There's nothing visible happening when a preacher says, "Your sins are forgiven." What does that even mean, to a crowd crammed into a tiny home in first-century Capernaum, or to us today? But if we hear someone command, "Get up and walk," and then someone actually gets up and walks, well then! In that case we will have witnessed a healing, with a verifiable, visible difference being made. The man couldn't walk, and now he can.

To the crowds gathered to hear Jesus, it probably does seem anti-climactic that all Jesus has done is declare that his sins are forgiven. At this point, they don't even fully know who he is, and they don't even think he has the authority to do that. It would seem easier to say, "Your sins are forgiven," which have no seeming effect, rather than heal a man's paralyzed legs. Miracles should have some showiness to them, shouldn't they?

We can't be faulted if we feel the same way in the confessional. We have done all this work—examined our consciences, named our sins aloud, and said we are sorry for what we have done wrong. This is far from easy, requiring humility and vulnerability, a desire for healing, and a willingness to seek it out. We pick ourselves up from the mud, push through the crowded thoughts of our minds and the hesitancy of our hearts, feel shame as we list what we have done, even as we know

Jesus is there with us in every moment. Not unlike these friends with their paralyzed pal, we break through the roof, drop down through the ceiling, just to get close to Jesus, hoping to be healed.

After all this effort, all this struggle, all this work, we hear, "Your sins are forgiven," and we just might be tempted to think, "But are they really?"

It Really Works

Up to this point, we've tried to more deeply understand how to just go get in line for Confession in the first place—a humble act admitting we have drifted from the Lord. And we've tried to unpack how to name our sins honestly and clearly and without hesitation, knowing that the Lord's mercy is not conditional and that when we ask for healing and beg for that mercy, we are drawn even closer to Jesus. In all of that, we know Jesus is lovingly waiting to receive us, see us as we are, look squarely upon our sins with us, and love us still.

We have to bust through walls, rip off roofs, fight through crowds around us and of our own making. Confession is not easy for us, and it is okay to say that. It is sometimes not pleasant, and none of us should assume it will be. No matter how good that mercy is in the end, or how relieved and healed we may feel when Confession is over, it is a mighty effort to go to and receive the mercy of God.

And so when we are done confessing our sins, after guidance and encouragement is offered by the priest to help us avoid sin in the future, and after we pray an Act of Contrition, expressing our sorrow and desire to turn away from sin, the priest lifts his right hand and offers the Prayer of Absolution, which can be found by scanning the QR code or visiting tinyurl.com/orderofpenance.

We've gotten up from the mud, covered in the grime of our own creation. We've pushed through crowds and reached out for help. We've sat in the shamefulness of all our wrongs and been seen for who we are: sinners who have fallen. We've dropped through the ceiling, paralyzed with our sins, hoping to walk again. And with a thirty-second prayer, said by a collared man in a purple stole with his hand raised in blessing, it's all gone. The sin is wiped away. The stain lifts off the fabric of our souls. The mud is washed off. The blood is dried up. Death is defeated. Shame is sent packing. Frail legs can hold our weight again. And if we sit there and think, *Wait, that's it? It's that easy?* no one would blame us. The Prayer of Absolution is almost comically simple, but it is a summation of all that has brought us to that beautiful moment when the Sacrament of Penance is completed.

Sin seems so complicated, when we're sinning and when we're examining our sin, and even as we confess it. We tied ourselves up in knots, the twists and turns of our failure and faults binding us up. The weight of what we've carried has crushed us into the ground. We are the prodigal son, the woman bleeding for twelve years, a desperate father begging for his daughter's life, a woman ashamed and outcast, and a paralyzed man with no way to get into the house. That mud and blood and illness and shamefulness and pain is so much to bear, it surely can't be *this* easy to just get rid of it. The stain will take far longer to wash out! Surely it will.

But the prodigal son got up. And the bleeding woman reached out. The father begged for help, and the outcast let herself be seen. The paralyzed man's friends ripped open the roof. Heavy sin and heavy shame and heavy burdens were healed and cast off each time because of a single act—getting up, reaching out, being honest, and getting close to Jesus.

Sin seems complicated, but it isn't. It's turning from the Lord, again and again. Confession seems hard. But it, too, isn't that hard, not in practice, not in reality. Jesus challenged the crowd in and surrounding the house in Capernaum to see the simplicity of it all. Their assumption then is ours today—healing should come in great dramatic miracles. Today, we sometimes think we need to beat our brow and be punished for our failures and faults. We may fear that a priest will scold or lecture us and slap a lengthy, difficult penance on us. And sometimes, in small corners of our hearts, in the deep recesses of our minds, we fear that the simple words "Your sins are forgiven" really are not true.

Christ Jesus, the Son of God and Word-Made-Flesh, is the Divine Physician who came to wrap our wounds and stop the bleeding. He comes today to heal us, and when we step into the confessional, with an examined conscience and a readiness to repent, the risen Christ is waiting for us in the person of the Church's priest. And he is ready to heal us, again and again.

Confession, in a way, is a moment to treat a stain of Red Dye 40 that's ruined the only school spirit shirt in the closet. Except we aren't a shirt with a penchant for holding red slushy in the fibers. We are an eternal, priceless child of God made in God's own image, beloved as sons and daughters who are welcomed home, no matter what. And in that confessional, the Divine Physician heals us. In that confessional, Christ, in the person of the priest, has the chance to treat the stains of sin and delete the marks upon us. It is in that confessional, with our heads bowed and sometimes our eyes closed, that the wounds are bound up, the bleeding stops, and we are set free. Our humble admissions of sin and the powerful Prayer of Absolution, together, remove the stain of sin.

Katie: Stain Treaters and Sin Deleters

Right before we left for Rose's First Reconciliation, Tommy did one last stain treatment on her spirit shirt. A few extra squirts couldn't hurt. And then, as Rose buckled into her booster seat and Tommy texted his and my parents about the dinner plans for after, I tossed the T-shirt into the washing machine. The red-dyed shirt would get its own load, on high heat, with color bleach and a deep-water soak. I asked my mother-in-law to toss it in the dryer when it was done, before they came to meet us at the restaurant.

Rose went in and out of the confessional, a kid transformed before and after. She slowly approached the cry room set up with a makeshift confessional, nervous because the windowed room meant she was in full view of a handful of her classmates as they waited their turns. But after a few minutes, she bounded out, seemingly floating on a cloud, a smile bigger than the one she had on her face as she sipped her slushy earlier that day.

She knelt down, prayed her penance, gave her teacher, Mrs. Lewis, a big hug, and then came over to us as we waited for her in a pew. "It's all gone, Mom!" She whisper-shouted. "All my sins are gone!"

"How's it feel, bud?" I asked her, beaming with pride.

"So good. I love it. Can we go get pizza now?" She's absolutely our kid, grateful to be forgiven and now wanting pizza to celebrate.

It was beautiful for Tommy and me to see her so confident and proud and clearly deeply moved by the reception of this remarkable grace for the first time. She had no doubts at all that her sins were gone, and she couldn't be happier. All through dinner, she kept reminding us how good she felt and how happy she was. "It's like the priest deleted all my sins, Mom! He's a sin deleter!" Those simple words of absolution made perfect sense in her young mind: Father said she was free, he sent her out with peace, and so, therefore, she was free and at peace. She had no worries that he'd go tell anyone what she'd done. No fear that he thought of her differently. No questioning whether she was or wasn't forgiven. She was free. The sins were gone. Treated. Deleted. Gone.

When we got home a couple of hours later, with squeaky-clean souls and bellies filled with pizza, we walked into the laundry room. Knowing it'd set her at ease from the drama of earlier in the day, I opened the dryer to see if the red dye had come out of her shirt. Rose saw it first, balled up in the middle of the dryer, the heat hitting us all as the light flickered.

"Is that the slushy shirt, Mom?" she sheepishly asked, her head hung low, a slight tremble in her little voice.

"Yeah, bud. It is," I said with a smile. Because I could tell, even as it was balled up, that the red stains had washed out. "Why don't you grab it?" I said.

Rose reached in and yanked the shirt out, clearly nervous she'd see on full display the shame of the exploding slushy. But as she unfurled it and realized it was good as new, clean and fresh and no red stains to be seen, she turned to me with the third brightest smile of the day. "It's all gone, Mom!" and she launched herself into my arms, wrinkling the hot shirt between us. "All the stains are gone!"

"They are, bud. Yes, they are." And in more than one way, all the stains were gone that day.

Thinking and Growing as Parents

Work through the following questions by yourself, and then use them to spark deeper conversation with your spouse, another important adult in your child's life, or the child you are helping to prepare for First Reconciliation.

1. Is there a moment, from any stage of your life, when you did something that you feared was unforgivable by God or someone you harmed? What do you remember about how you felt about this "permanent stain" you felt you were carrying?

2. What stands out to you most in the Prayer of Absolution? (See page 50.) Is there a phrase that really catches your attention?

3. Is there anything in the Prayer of Absolution that challenges or troubles you? Anything that's tough to believe or accept?

4. Do you remember a really good Confession you've made before? What do you remember about it that made it a "good Confession"? Was there anything that you did, or the priest did, that was helpful in your healing?

5. If you had to describe how you feel in the confessional when you hear the words "Your sins are forgiven," what would you say?

Growing Together as Parents and Children

This step or spiritual habit is longer than the others in this book. Our hope is that you dig deep here with your child. Perhaps divide the conversation questions into two or three parts and discuss at different times. This script is a good tool to return to over and over with your child. Maybe bookmark it.

We knew there were three big things we needed to prepare our daughter for when it came to receiving the Sacrament of Reconciliation for the first time. We needed to talk about examining our consciences (see the appendix for examinations for adults, children, and families) and help her make time to pray. We needed to teach her the Act of Contrition and explain what it meant. And we needed to prepare her to hear the priest's Prayer of Absolution and help her fully understand the power of those words and receive their healing grace into her heart.

Sample Script

Pray the Act of Contrition together, and then talk together using the questions that follow. There are a few common versions of this prayer, so if this one is different from the one your parish or school or religious-education class is using, please use the one with which you are most familiar. You can always pray the one found in The Order for Reconciling Individual Penitents, *which you bookmarked or printed. It can be found by scanning the QR code or visiting tinyurl.com/orderofpenance.*

O my God, I am heartily sorry for having offended you,
and I detest all my sins because of your just punishments,
but most of all because they offend you, my God,
who art all good and deserving of all my love.
I firmly resolve with the help of your grace to sin no more
and to avoid the near occasion of sin.
Amen.

1. What jumps out to you in the prayer? After listening to it one time, what phrase or word stands out in your head? Why?

2. What do you think it means to be heartily sorry? Have you ever been really sorry for something you did, maybe with a sibling, or a classmate, or your parents?

3. Do you know what *detest* means? What are some other words with nearly the same meaning?

4. When we say we *detest* all our sins, that means we really dislike them, and when we dislike something, and we know something is wrong, we want to get rid of it. Can you think of any sins you want to get rid of?

5. Have you done anything that you are ready to tell Jesus you are sorry for? How about we talk about that?

6. It hurts our relationship with God when we choose to do things in a way that pulls us away from him. Let's name some things we know are wrong and yet sometimes do. Is it easy for you to sometimes do wrong things? Why do you think that is?

7. In the Act of Contrition, we pray that God is all good and deserving of all our love. When have you felt God's love? When have you seen God make a difference in your life? Do you believe God is deserving of all your love?

8. In this prayer, we claim that we firmly resolve not to sin again. This means we are making a commitment always to try to do the right things. We choose to live as God wants for us. Have you ever resolved to do something different or new? What did you do to be successful in keeping that resolution?

9. What things in your life sometimes make you want to do something you know is wrong? How can you get rid of those things in your life?

56   First Reconciliation and Beyond

10. Read the Prayer of Absolution together (from *The Order for Reconciling Individual Penitents*, which you bookmarked or printed). How do you think it will feel to hear those words for the first time? Are you nervous? Excited? Confused? Worried? Happy? How do you feel hearing those words right now?

11. Do you believe Jesus can forgive your sins? Why or why not?

12. Who has forgiven you before? How did that feel? What did you think about receiving their forgiveness?

13. Have you felt peaceful before? What helped you feel that way? What was happening around you that helped you be at peace?

14. When we go to Confession, we are not going to be punished. We are going to Confession because we want to be forgiven and because we know Jesus is waiting to give us his mercy. We will be pardoned. We will be at peace. Are you excited to experience that for the first time, and many more times in the future?

Praying as a Family

Wrap up your conversation in prayer. You might pray spontaneously by saying aloud to God whatever is on your heart and encourage your child or the children with you to do the same. Or pray the simple prayer we offer here. Or pray in both ways!

> O God,
> we are sorry for what we have done.
> Help us to turn to you so that we can sin no more
> and live in your love.
> Amen.

5

Jesus Has Something for You

Joining Our Stories to the Church's Story

Katie: Something for You

In May 2020, as the world was closed during the COVID-19 pandemic, I found myself pregnant and on modified bedrest with our second daughter, Clare. I was stuck at home like the rest of the world, scared about the future, and worried I'd get sick. I sat around watching ridiculous reality television, reading through our shelves of books, scrolling social media until my thumbs cramped. My career traveling and speaking around the world was on hold, and my motivation for anything creative or productive was gone. My optimism, which, let's be real, wasn't entirely off the charts prior to the pandemic, had all but disappeared. I was miserable, lonely, anxious, and sinking into despair. If we're being honest, I was a little angry, mostly with God.

On a particularly low day, as I was lying in bed staring at the wall, wondering if life would ever get back to normal, my husband came into our bedroom and told me it was time to get up and go do something.

"Anything," he begged me. He knew I was struggling. "Go walk around the block. The doctor said you're allowed to walk."

"No," I muttered back.

"Or go drive to Target and just sit in the parking lot and make a pick-up order," he pleaded.

"I can do it from my phone, and you can go get it with Rose," I retorted back.

"Katie!" he bellowed into the dark room. "Please! This isn't good for Clare!" and he stormed out. Then, as if on cue, the baby inside kicked and stretched as if in agreement.

Tommy was right. I needed to go do something, anything, even if I had zero motivation to do so. The world had stopped, and much of everyday life with it, while a new life continued to grow inside me. So, I threw on halfway decent clothes, got into the car, and found myself driving down Lake Street, thinking I'd hang a left and head to the store. But instead, I went straight, muscle memory and zoned-out driving leading me to the parking lot of Our Lady Queen of Heaven Catholic Church. Parked outside the perpetual Eucharistic adoration chapel, I debated with myself. On the one hand, they'd moved the chapel to a larger space so people could sit far enough apart from one another and be safer. On the other hand, it wasn't other people I wanted to be distant from. Truthfully, I had no desire to sit in front of the Eucharist or be anywhere around Jesus. But I was in the parking lot—somehow, I'd driven myself there—so after a few minutes of self-loathing and pity, I went inside.

The chapel was empty, just one other person praying right in front. I slipped into the back row, wobbled my pregnant self down onto my knees, looked up at the monstrance holding the Eucharist, and sighed. It was a deep, guttural sigh, louder than I intended it to be, and as the other woman glanced back in my direction, I scolded myself for being a distraction to this lovely person who was probably less than thrilled with someone else disturbing her holy hour. The chapel had only just recently reopened, with very strict guidelines and sign-ups, and here I was, pregnant and sighing and probably breaking the rules.

I closed my eyes and tried to pray, to no avail. I sat down, keeping my eyes closed, hoping maybe just looking like I was praying would lead to prayer. I fidgeted in my seat, crossing and uncrossing my ankles repeatedly, literally twiddling my thumbs as I felt the crushing weight of the silence and my empty mind and angry heart.

"Excuse me," a voice whispered. I cracked open my eyes and saw that the woman in the front row was trying to get my attention. "Do you plan on being here awhile?" she whispered.

"Uh . . ." I tried to think of an answer. Did I plan on staying? I had shown up, after all, and it wasn't like I had anything better to do. I glanced down at my watch—11:15. I was staying for fifteen minutes, and then at 11:30 I was going to leave, go through the Chick-fil-A drive-thru, and treat myself to a frozen lemonade, as was my right as a sulking pregnant lady.

"I have to run, but Father usually comes at noon, so if you could just finish out the hour, that'd be great," she quickly said. And before I knew it, she was up and out the door, leaving me alone in the Eucharistic adoration chapel, sitting in the back row, pregnant and out of the house for the first time in a week in the middle of a global pandemic.

Welp, I thought to myself. And then I looked up, stared squarely at the monstrance (sacred vessel holding the consecrated host), and said, "Just you and me now, Jesus." I crossed my arms, harrumphed like an angry cartoon character, and closed my eyes again.

Five minutes passed. I prayed not at all. Another ten minutes went by. I had nothing to say to the Lord in those moments. A few more minutes, and I got squirmy in my seat. "What?" I sarcastically tossed in the direction of the monstrance. "Do you want me to tell you what's wrong?" I was putting on my best sassy teenager impression. "It all sucks, okay? Just all of it. How could you?" The next thing I knew, I was letting Jesus have it.

All my anger and hurt and frustration and fear fell out of my mouth as I just laid it all out for the Lord. We'd been trying to get pregnant for a year, and it finally happened five days into 2020, and then the world just closed? I worked nonstop to build a reputation and a career and the skills to travel around the world and speak, and then everything just stopped? My daughter was thriving in pre-K-2, Tommy was finally loving teaching in the classroom, and now it was just all on hold? Everything came out, this anger I'd been clinging to, this blame I needed to place at Jesus's feet. This was his fault, my suffering was his doing, and he deserved to hear it.

I wore myself out, the frustrated words and eventually the tears exhausting me, until finally I just sat there, shoulders slumped. I hadn't brought anything with me into the chapel, when usually I had a Bible, book, rosary, and journal. My phone was in the cupholder in the car. I was stuck, all by myself in the adoration chapel, unable to leave the Blessed Sacrament alone.

Confession would be nice right about now, I thought to myself, sheepishly looking up at the Lord. It had been a while since I'd gone, and I had certainly just unleashed enough vitriol to warrant reconciling with the God I'd come to resent.

The silence of the chapel was deafening. "What?" I said out loud. "What do you want from me?" I said to the Lord, our unending staring contest annoying me. "What do you want from me?" I said again. Because truly, in that moment, I felt as if I'd done all I could do, and still, this was the end result. For a third time, louder than before, I said out loud, "What. Do. You. Want. From. Me?" The silence thundered.

I've only truly felt the presence of God in my life a handful of times, that deep awareness that God is right there, right beside me. I don't have any scientific proof of this, of course, but I think that when we feel God's presence, everyone has a different sensation alerting us to this presence. For some, maybe God is present in a refreshing breeze, cooling them down. For others, maybe God is in the bright light shining down on them, guiding them forward. For me, God's tangible presence feels like velvet, wrapping around my shoulders, the weight of the fabric settling on me as the Lord speaks.

"I don't want anything from you," I heard in my heart. I looked up, staring at the monstrance, gazing upon our Eucharistic Lord, wondering if it was really Christ speaking to me. "I don't want anything from you," I heard again.

Well, fine, I thought to myself. "I don't want anything from you," I heard again, clear as a bell. "I want something *for* you."

I felt as if a great whooshing washed over my mind, almost as if my hair had blown back just as the velvet weighed heavier on me. "I want something *for* you," I heard one more time.

For me? What could I possibly deserve? What had I earned? What did the Lord have for me, the whining, sinful woman who had no desire to spend any time with him except to list off her complaints and frustrations? What could Christ possibly have for me?

And right on cue, as I sat there stunned by this quiet revelation from the Lord, the side door of the adoration chapel opened, and in walked my parish priest.

Katie: A Gift for Me

Equally shocked to see me, Father glanced around the chapel, looking for the regularly assigned adorer. "She had to go," I quickly said. "I told her I'd stay until you got here," and then I caught myself. No, I hadn't. But I was there.

"That's alright," Father said back. He stood at the door, waiting to fully come into the chapel. "Do you need anything?" he asked, staring at me, the evidence of my tears clearly on my face. "Are you okay?" he gently added.

"I'm fine," I said, clearly not.

"Okay." Father walked to the front row. "Well, I'm here if you need anything, like Confession," and he sat down, his back to me, as he reached into his pocket and pulled out his purple travel stole and placed it around his neck. It's like he knew.

I glanced back up at the monstrance, nearly laughing and rolling my eyes at the same time. *Good one, God,* I sheepishly thought. *You have a priest for me? Show-off.*

"Actually," I quickly said. "Could you? Hear it? If that's okay?"

Father turned around, three rows ahead of me, a huge smile breaking out across his face, visible even behind the cloth mask covering his mouth. "I'd love to," he said.

As I confessed my sins, which seemed numerous and relentlessly shameful as they poured out of me, one after the other, I suddenly felt as if I was floating. A pregnant woman getting lightheaded is cause for concern, but I knew it wasn't a blood-sugar crash or early labor. I felt lighter as the sins seemingly lifted off me, one by one spoken aloud, as the muck and mud, the bleeding and hurt, the shame and guilt—all of it sloughed off, and I could see redemption was near. I paused as I listed off my last sin, silence filling the chapel.

"Is that everything?" Father asked.

"Yes," I murmured back, staring at the back of his head and up at the monstrance all at the same time.

It was beautiful and also a bit jarring. There was Jesus, present in the Eucharist held in the monstrance, set atop the altar. And there was the priest, hearing my Confession, representing the same Jesus I was gazing upon, offering me the loving mercy of God through the ministry of the church.

"Jesus has so much for you, Katie," Father began.

What did he just say?

"And we have to *want* to receive what he wants to give, because *He has so much good for us.*"

The words rang through my head, and the velvet warmth seemed to gently squeeze tighter around my shoulders.

"Can you make your Act of Contrition?" Father asked.

"Oh my God, I am heartily sorry for having offended you, and I detest all my sins, because of your just punishment." My voice hitched. "But most of all because I offend you, my God, who are all good and deserving of all my love." Is he deserving of all my love? Yes. Had I given it? No. Not at all.

This is at the heart of Confession. This is what's in the midst of the remarkable gift of the Sacrament of Reconciliation. God is deserving of all our love, and he so longs to freely give his love to us. But when we sin, we drift away from, reject, and resist love, both our love to give and his love to receive. As that happens, we become hardened, ashamed of what we've done, at times angry with him and ourselves, but most significantly, we become distant and isolated.

The prodigal son was alone in the mud, broken and hungry. The hemorrhaging woman was bleeding in isolation, an outcast in her hurt. The woman at the well was hiding at the hottest part of the day, ashamed of all she'd done. The paralyzed man was on a mat on the roof, unable to walk, far from Jesus.

But the prodigal son got up and was joyously greeted by his father. The hemorrhaging woman reached out and as instantly healed. The woman at the well was seen fully by Jesus. The paralyzed man was placed before Jesus and got up and walked. They were healed, each and every one, as they drew near to Jesus. And that is all we are doing in Confession: We are drawing close to Jesus, receiving his love, and accepting the mercy he has *for us.*

I concluded the prayer, "I firmly resolve, with the help of your grace, to sin no more, and to avoid the near occasion of sin." Then, sighing deeply I breathed out, "Amen," and waited.

From the front row of the empty adoration chapel, Father turned slightly toward me, in the back row, and raised his hand in my direction and prayed the Prayer of Absolution.

> God, the Father of mercies,
> through the Death and Resurrection of his Son
> has reconciled the world to himself. . . .

For me, I thought. *He reconciled the world* for me.

I absolve you from your sins. . . .

For me. I'm absolved, forgiven, set free. His mercy is for me.
Confession may, at times, seem rote or overly legalistic. It may seem
like a chore. If we aren't careful, we can easily grow to resent it as a task
rather than receive it as gift. The Sacrament of Reconciliation is the gift
by which we are drawn back into the loving arms of our merciful God.
It is a gift by which we are healed, clothed in dignity as relationships
are restored. It is a gift by which we are enabled to go forth, confident
that we have not drifted so far that we can't come back home.

Learning from Scripture

Katie: What God Has Done for You

My penance that day of the unexpected COVID Confession was simple.
I was asked to read Luke chapter 8 and pick one of the healing stories
there that stood out to me. "They're all very meaningful, but I think
you'll particularly like the story of the Gerasene demoniac," Father
had told me.

I knew the story, somewhat: when Jesus made pigs fly. Why would
this story stand out to me, at this time? Luke 8 contains the raising
of Jairus's daughter from the dead, the healing of the hemorrhaging
woman, the calming of the storm with the apostles in the boat. Surely
one of those stories would stand out to me more, considering I was a
somewhat lifeless, always nauseated woman who was stuck in the storm
of a global pandemic at that very moment. Possessed men with no name
were not front of mind for me. But I went home, got out my dusty Bible,
and read the story of the Gerasene demoniac (Luke 8:26–39).

This is one of Jesus's more dramatic exorcisms, involving an
unnamed man possessed by demons, living among the tombs. He is all
alone. He has no home, no life, no clothes even. He is utterly destitute
and possessed. And he has been healed before. Luke's gospel tells us
that this man had been cleansed of unclean spirits many times before,
and he would still end up wandering around the deserted places, ter-
rorizing others or himself.

This man with no name, no home, no community, and no prospects
sees Jesus. And Jesus sees him wandering, possessed, naked, and afraid.

Jesus casts the demons out of this man, and an unfortunate herd of swine fall off a cliff, into a lake, and drown.

At this point in the story, we might chuckle. Jesus is nothing if not occasionally comical. Make those pigs fly, Lord! But the pig shepherds (swineherds) see it all and immediately go tell everyone that their pigs are gone and that Jesus, along with the possessed man, is possibly to blame. So, crowds of people come out to see what's happened. There's Jesus, talking to their friendly neighborhood demoniac, who is sitting at his feet. The nameless man, now dispossessed of the demons, is described as "clothed and in his right mind" in Luke 8:35.

He's clothed now, when just a few verses before he was described as naked. Jesus has cast out the demons from the possessed man. He sat and listened to the man and cared for him as no one has before. It isn't out of the realm of possibility that Jesus would've taken off his outer garment, a mantle worn as sort of an overcoat or jacket, and wrapped it around the man he had just healed. Where else would the clothing have come from? Where else could this man find healing? Only with Jesus.

Jesus provides for the greatest needs *and* the immediate needs. He heals the ailment, and he heals the nakedness. He restores the man's soul and cares for his body. This nameless, naked, possessed man is restored to life, then clothed, and then heard. Nothing for him will ever be the same.

Crowds from the entire region of the Gerasenes show up to see what's happening, and when they see the possessed man now clothed and in his right mind, they are flummoxed and scared. Who could do this? Why would this happen? How? When they realize it must've been Jesus, someone they do not know or understand, they tell him to leave. Their fear overtakes any sense of wonder or awe, and Jesus knows when he's not welcome. As he prepares to leave, the healed man, who still has no name, begs to go with him.

That shouldn't be too surprising. Jesus has given him freedom from demons and wrapped his own cloak around the man's naked body. Everything in this man's life has changed, forever. He is ready to leave it all behind to go with Jesus. But Jesus doesn't let him. He tells the freshly healed man to stay, and in fact, Jesus gives him a very clear mission: "Return home and recount what God has done for you."

Wearing Jesus's cloak and filled with the grace of Jesus acting in his life, a man whose name we do not know goes back to a town filled with people who have rejected him and Jesus to proclaim the goodness of God. Now, what he has to proclaim is remarkably personal. What God has done *for him* is no small thing. He has been healed. He has been set free. He has been provided for. He has been restored and his entire life is different, because of what God has done *for him*. So, he goes and tells everyone about that, holding nothing back, proclaiming with joy and fervor the gift he has been given.

Tommy: Confession Is Not Just for You

We pulled into the parking lot of St. Margaret Catholic Church at 3:20 in the afternoon on Christmas Eve, in the typical frantic fashion with which we've grown familiar. Clare's shoe had fallen off, Katie discovered a stain on my sweater right as she got out of the van, and I was wearing mismatched socks. But Rose was calm, cool, and collected as we walked into the church, and she turned to me and confidently announced, "I want to get in line for Confession."

"Are they hearing Confessions right now, buddy?" I gently asked her. Christmas Eve Mass surely requires some intense sacristy prep, so I was certain our pastor and only parish priest wasn't sitting in the confessional before the first of the many Masses he was about to preside over for the next two days. But as we looked over to the back left corner of the church, the red light was on over the confessional door, and two people were sitting in the back pew, waiting their turn.

Rose happily trotted off, sat down, and waited patiently for her turn. Katie, Clare, and I walked off to go get seated in our usual pew, and as we situated ourselves, I glanced back to make sure Rose was still okay. She had a huge smile on her face, with just one person now in front of her in the line, and as she noticed me looking at her, she waved me over.

I leaned over to Katie, who was helping Clare with her jacket, and whispered, "Do you mind if I go to Confession too?"

"Go ahead," she quickly said back.

I got up to go join Rose, who seemed delighted beyond compare as I sat down next to her. "I get to go to Confession for Jesus's birthday!" she excitedly whispered to me, and I teared up a bit as I looked down at her, a little seven-year-old, second-grade girl who could barely contain her joy at getting to receive the Sacrament of Reconciliation for the second time in her life.

It'd only been six days since her first Confession, and I wasn't even sure what she'd examined in her conscience that had prompted her to want to confess. To be fair, I thought she probably just wanted to go because she could. And as I looked down at her, clutching her children's missalette and the rosary ring her teacher had given her just a few days before, I recognized a stillness and peace in my daughter that I hadn't ever seen before.

Rose is a wiggler. Ever since she was a baby, she has rarely been still. At just three weeks old, Katie and I learned she couldn't stand to be swaddled, and so we set her little arms free from the Velcro swaddles so she could stretch and flail to her heart's content. The night we did that was the first time she slept for longer than two hours at a time. She is always shaking her foot or bouncing her knee or moving her fingers. In a lot of ways, her wiggling makes her *her*. It hasn't bothered us, it has never been a behavioral or classroom issue at school, and so Rose's little bit of motion and movement was never a cause for concern.

But as we sat there in the back pew, waiting to go to Confession on Christmas Eve, Rose was still. Her foot wasn't tapping; her knee wasn't bouncing. Her hands were clasped together, eyes closed, and I could tell her breathing had slowed to a gentle rhythm. She was at peace, comforted by the knowledge that in mere moments she'd receive the sacramental grace of God's forgiveness.

It was precisely because it was so new to her, this remarkable outward sign of God's enduring mercy, that she was so excited. And in knowing that this was something she could receive again and again, she'd found a stillness she'd never known before. In that moment, my daughter was still and knew that God was near.

The confessional door opened, and Rose stood up. As she stepped out of the pew, she turned to me, another big smile on her face, and said, "Oh, I can't wait!" and she bounced off as if little wings had sprouted from her ankles.

There are moments when you're proud of your children—when they nail their piece at the piano recital or come home with a great report card or when they're eminently kind to someone else in a challenging situation. But then, as I was slowly discovering, there are moments when the pride and joy is not sparked because of anything my child has done for herself, but because of what is happening within her heart and mind because of God's grace. Rose was coming to know God's love in a new way. She was being healed, seen fully, loved completely, pulled into the warm embrace of the Lord. My child was receiving the love of the Lord, embracing it in her heart, and as her father I was proud beyond compare to know that she now knew *our* Father in this new way.

Watching my child discover the abundant love and mercy of the Lord through the Sacrament of Reconciliation was a gift because it was reminding me of God's love and mercy that was meant for me too. She wanted to go to Confession, and it prompted me to go too. She was excited for the gift of forgiveness, and it prompted me to seek that forgiveness too. She was transformed by what the Lord had done for her, and just like the nameless man possessed by demons who was freed from his oppression, she was giving a vibrant witness of the freedom only Jesus can give. Her Confession wasn't just for her; it was for our entire family, near and far, because our seven-year-old was discovering the remarkable joy of the sacrament for the first time. And she was telling and showing us what the Lord had done for her, reminding us that all of that grace was for us too.

Go Home

When we receive the abundant mercy of the Lord, when we are freed of our sins and healed in powerful ways through the Sacrament of Reconciliation, we, like the Gerasene demoniac, are called to go home. Like him, we may want to just stay right there, in the church, in the pew, with the priest, in the privacy and quiet of the moment of being absolved or set free from our sins. The confessional is safe. The pew is easy. The church is where this mercy was given to us, so why would we ever want to leave? But we are sent home to go and tell what the Lord has done for us. We are asked to go on mission, too, not keeping the joy of this forgiveness to ourselves.

We go back home, to the kitchen with dirty dishes in the sink and mounds of laundry. We go back home, to bedrooms filled with clutter and the home office never organized enough. We go back home, to the place we know best with the people we hopefully love most. We go home, changed forever by the loving mercy of the Lord, and we are asked to love others in the same way we have been loved by Jesus.

We have been forgiven, and we are challenged to forgive. We have been loved, and we are commanded to love. We have been changed forever, and we get to invite people into this transformation that comes when we encounter the Lord in Confession.

Confession doesn't happen *to* us. It happens *for* us, and *in* us, and the greatest acts we can ever hope to do with the grace of the sacrament are to sin no more and to challenge others to do the same.

Walking with a child to their First Reconciliation, helping them begin to know the mercy of the Father, is a privilege and gift beyond compare. It's a privilege because we get to help someone know God's healing love in this way for the first time. And it is a gift because we are reminded of all the ways God has loved and healed us in our own lives.

Thinking and Growing as Parents

Work through the following questions by yourself, and then use them to spark deeper conversation with your spouse, another important adult in your child's life, or the child you are helping to prepare for First Reconciliation.

1. Have you ever felt isolated or alone, due to your own sin or maybe the sins of others? What was it like to feel alone?

2. Who has helped you more fully understand or appreciate the Sacrament of Reconciliation? What did they say or do to teach you about Confession?

3. Have you ever had the chance to teach or share about Confession with anyone before? What did you say or do? How did it feel to share about the Sacrament of Reconciliation with others?

4. Have you ever been hesitant or scared to talk about the Sacrament of Reconciliation? If so, why do you think that was?

5. Have you ever been excited or really ready to share with another person your experience of the Sacrament of Reconciliation? What made you ready for that?

Growing Together as Parents and Children

Use the material that follows to talk with your child about what the Bible story tells them about Jesus. Listen and learn from your child. Share with him or her what you think of the story and who you know Jesus to be in your own life, particularly about how you have grown to know Jesus better in the Sacrament of Reconciliation or simply in using this book.

Sample Script

Read Luke 8:26–39, the story of the Gerasene demoniac, then discuss these questions:

1. The Gerasene Demoniac yells at Jesus when he first sees him and asks him why he's there. He says he is "tormented" by Jesus being there. Jesus is upsetting him. Why do you think he was so upset? Why do you think he might have been living all alone for so long?

2. Jesus heals the man and drives out the unclean spirits. He helps the man feel better; he helps him feel peaceful. Think of a time in your life when you were feeling bad and then got better. What happened? What helped you feel better? Who helped you feel better?

3. When the townspeople find out that Jesus has healed the possessed man in the Bible story, they are afraid, and so they tell Jesus to leave. Why do you think they're afraid of Jesus at that moment?

4. When Jesus goes to leave, the Gerasene man wants to go with Jesus and remain with him. Why do you think the man who was healed wants to go with Jesus?

5. Jesus doesn't let the man go with him but instead tells him to go home and tell everyone about what's happened for him. Jesus asks him to go share with others how he has been healed. Have you ever told others about Jesus? What did you say? Has anyone ever shared Jesus with you?

When we go to Confession, we know that everything is about to change: We are going to be healed by Jesus, because we are willing to admit when we have sinned and to ask Jesus to forgive us. Jesus really, truly, and without delay forgives us. He wipes away the stain of sin. He tells us that what we have done is forgiven, which means he does not hold it against us.

Imagine that there's a stain on a shirt, and it is put through the washing machine with a stain treater. When the stain comes out, we can wear the shirt again with pride. The stain is all gone. If you knew there was something out there that got rid of all the worst stains—grass stains, juice or slushy stains, chocolate stains, dirt stains—would you want to tell everyone about this great stain treater? Would you share the good news that you found something that works to remove stains? Or would you just keep it to yourself?

Praying as a Family

Wrap up your conversation in prayer. You might pray spontaneously by saying aloud to God whatever is on your heart and encourage your child or the children with you to do the same. Or pray the simple prayer we offer here. Or pray in both ways!

Lord Jesus,
show us what you have for us,
and help us to be open
to receiving your good gifts.
Amen.

Epilogue

A Louisiana Blizzard

We received a great grace and seemingly impossible gift the week we finished writing this book. On Tuesday, January 21, 2025, our small town of Lake Charles, Louisiana, woke up to our first-ever blizzard warning issued from the National Weather Service. For nearly twelve hours, snow fell in Lake Charles. We recorded seven inches of snow in our own yard, and for two full days, we built snowmen, sledded (as best we could, with cookie sheets and laundry baskets) down tiny hills, and had snowball fights up and down our street. It was a ridiculously amazing few days, as we kept looking out the window stunned that there was snow on the ground.

As we were all dozing on the couch at the end of our first-ever family snow day, a movie playing in the background, a fire crackling in the fireplace, Rose leaned over and whispered, "Mom, today was perfect."

"It was pretty close to perfect," I said back.

"But, Mom, I need to go to Confession as soon as the snow melts and we can drive again."

I'd watched her all day and hadn't really noticed anything that would be "Confession worthy" in her behavior. "What do you mean, bud?" I asked.

"Well . . . I got a little jealous today, and I said something unkind to Clare, and I hid the remote so she couldn't change the show we were watching, and I just need to tell Jesus I'm sorry and hear him say he still loves me," she blurted out really quickly. "That's all."

She was sitting in the same spot she'd sat in when I'd caught her on YouTube all those months ago, but at that moment, her little face didn't turn bright red from shame. Her voice didn't quiver as she was very honest. She knew she needed to go to Confession, she knew what would happen when she went, and she knew Jesus was waiting, right in the confessional, ready to give her his love and mercy.

The snow would eventually melt. We'll likely never see a blizzard in Louisiana again, at least not in our lifetimes. We'll never forget the magic and beauty of that day, fresh snowfall in our front yard, only twenty-seven miles from the Gulf Coast. But even more beautiful was the sight of my daughter, confident and hopeful in the mercy and for-giveness of Jesus that she finds, again and again, in the Sacrament of Reconciliation.

Acknowledgments

We're so very grateful for the guidance, editing, and hard work of Eileen Ponder, the best editor we know and love, and the amazing visionaries at Ave Maria Press. Y'all are truly the best in the biz, and we love writing books with you.

Many thanks go to our parents, Sandy and Tom McGrady and Marie and Garland Prejean, who provided countless hours of childcare and grandparent time so that we could escape parenting duties to do some essential writing.

To the good priests, of all ages, ranks, and locations, that we know and love: You have heard our Confessions, offered us advice, and loved our family, and we are so grateful for your fatherly love.

And to our girls, Bud and Bear: You are both the lights of our lives, and being your parents is the greatest honor and joy. We love you.

Appendix

Helpful Tools for Making a Good Confession

Scripture Passages

Sometimes, it helps to read scripture when we examine our consciences. When we read scripture, we are changed and become different. We are touched, changed forever, by the words of our Lord, and when we read the Bible before going to Confession, we can more clearly see how we have, or have not, made room for the Lord in our lives. Here is a list of passages from scripture that are particularly helpful to read when making an examination of conscience.

- The Prodigal Son: Luke 15:11–32
- The Woman at the Well: John 4
- The Beatitudes: Matthew 5:3–12
- A Penitential Psalm: Psalm 51
- The Ten Commandments: Exodus 20
- Peter, Do You Love Me?: John 21:15–19
- The Good Shepherd: Luke 15:1–7 or John 10
- Jesus and the Good Thief: Luke 23:39–43
- The Healing of the Leper: Matthew 8:1–4
- The Raising of Lazarus: John 11

Examinations of Conscience

Find a quiet place, and try to silence your head and your heart. Take three deep breaths, close your eyes, and try to picture Jesus sitting next to you. What does Jesus look like to you? Is he smiling at you, or maybe reaching out to hold your hand? Is he saying something to you? Do you have anything you'd like to say to him?

For Adults

1. Have I replaced God's rule over my life with commitments, things, or people?
2. Are there forces or voices that I've allowed to hold my heart and will captive from doing the will of God?
3. Have I taken a gift from God in my life and elevated it above God himself? Have I made things, circumstances, work, money, influence, or power an idol?
4. Do I have any habitual patterns that do not allow my heart to be free to choose God? What am I doing more than I am paying attention to the Lord?
5. Does the story I tell myself about my faith match my actions and attitudes? Have I been "Christian" in name only?
6. Is my heart fully committed to prayer? Do I listen to God's voice or just talk over him?
7. Do I give enough time in my day and week to prayer and works of service for the Lord?
8. Have I placed burdens on others that have made it harder for them to listen to God's voice?
9. Have I been a source of joy, peace, and mercy for my family?
10. Do my choices reflect the virtues my parents and elders have tried to teach me?
11. Do I listen to voices of authority and guidance in my life? Do I obey rightly given instructions and commands?
12. Have I judged someone harshly for behaviors that I then justify for myself?
13. Have I let anger toward others fester in my heart?
14. Have I treated my spouse with kindness, compassion, and love?
15. Have I given something or someone more attention in place of my spouse?
16. Do I take credit for things I didn't do?
17. Have I been selfish in the use of my time?
18. Have I spoken poorly of anyone behind their back? Have I spread falsehoods, rumors, or lies?

19. Did I attempt to make myself appear to be better than anyone in the eyes of others?
20. Have I taken for granted any gift from God in my life?
21. Have I misused resources, especially those I have worked hard to earn?
22. Have I been disrespectful to or frivolous with my life or the lives of others?
23. Am I resentful or ungrateful for my present circumstances?

For Kids

1. Do I try to listen for God's voice when I make tough choices?
2. Do I start and end my days with prayer?
3. Did I use unkind or hateful language?
4. Would a total stranger know I was Catholic if they heard the words I say?
5. Have I gone to church every Sunday and Holy Day of Obligation?
6. Have I taken time to notice and thank God for the gifts around me?
7. Have I respected all my family members and treated them with respect?
8. Have I complained about something my parents told me to do?
9. Did I make anyone feel unloved or unwanted?
10. Did I do anything that has harmed someone?
11. Do I treat everyone like a brother or sister in Christ?
12. Did I honor God with the choices I made with my body?
13. Have I hurt anyone physically? Have I said something that hurt someone's feelings?
14. Did I take anything that did not belong to me?
15. Have I stolen attention from others?
16. Did I talk about other people behind their back?
17. Did I try to make myself look better than someone else?
18. Have I hidden the truth to not get in trouble?
19. Have I been ungrateful for the things I have?
20. Did I compare myself to others?

For Families

1. Have we made anything more important than God?
2. Did we take time to pray together?
3. Have we been ashamed to say we are Catholic?

4. Did we make sacrifices for one another?
5. Did we fail to act like Jesus toward one another?
6. Have we gone through the motions with our family prayers?
7. Did we make it to Mass every Sunday?
8. Have we been loving to one another?
9. Have we been helpful to one another?
10. Did we respond to one another with patience and respect?
11. Have we responded with anger instead of understanding?
12. Has anyone in our family felt unloved or left out?
13. Did we fail to treat someone in our family as if they were Jesus himself?
14. Have we used our bodies to glorify God?
15. Did we borrow or take something without asking?
16. Were we generous with our family money and possessions?
17. Did we tear someone down to build ourselves up?
18. Have we been ignorant of God's grace in our family?
19. Did we forget to thank God for what we have before asking for or buying something we don't?

Katie Prejean McGrady is host of the *Ave Explores* podcast and *The Katie McGrady Show* on Sirius XM's The Catholic Channel. She is an international speaker, the author of *Room 24: Adventures of a New Evangelist* and *Follow: Your Lifelong Adventure with Jesus*, and the coauthor of *Lent: One Day at a Time for Catholic Teens* and *Advent and Christmas: One Day at a Time for Catholic Teens*.

Prejean McGrady also serves as host of the *Like a Mother* podcast and cohost of *Family Mass Prep* on the Hallow app. She writes for several outlets, including Blessed is She, *Our Sunday Visitor*, and *Aleteia*, and contributes coverage on the Vatican and Church news to CNN. Prejean McGrady has spoken at the National Catholic Youth Conference, Steubenville Youth Conferences, and the Los Angeles Religious Education Congress, as well as in dioceses and parishes throughout the world.

Prejean McGrady earned a theology degree from the University of Dallas.

She lives in Lake Charles, Louisiana, with her husband Tommy and their children.

Website: katieprejeanmcgrady.com
Facebook: katiepmcgrady
Instagram: @katiepmcgrady
X: @katiepmcgrady

Tommy McGrady is a biology teacher at Lake Charles College Prep in Louisiana, cohost of *Family Mass Prep* on the Hallow app, and a parish coach for the Accompaniment Project with the National Federation for Catholic Youth Ministry. He is the author of Life Teen's *Unleashed: Men of Scripture* and coauthor of *Lent: One Day at a Time for Catholic Teens* and *Advent and Christmas: One Day at a Time for Catholic Teens.* He has spoken at a number of youth rallies, youth ministry trainings, and diocesan events throughout the country.

In 2016, McGrady earned a distinguished young alumni award from Eastern University, where he earned a bachelor's degree in biology in 2010. In 2023, he completed his master's degree in educational administration. McGrady previously served as the coordinator of youth and young adult ministry in the Diocese of Scranton and as a campus minister and theology teacher at St. Louis Catholic High School in Lake Charles, Louisiana.

He lives in Lake Charles, Louisiana, with his wife Katie and their children.

Facebook: Tommy McGrady
Instagram: @tmcgrady25
X: @tmcgrady25

Did You Love This Book?
DON'T STOP HERE. *Go Beyond!*

Explore more with a special video series created by the authors—
designed for parents, educators, and kids!

Watch together as the McGrady's bring key themes
from the book to life with **practical insights**, **real-life stories**,
and **spiritual encouragement** for families.

SCAN HERE TO WATCH NOW.

Follow on Hallōw

You can also find their exclusive series on Hallow, the **#1 Catholic
prayer and meditation app**, where they offer faith-filled reflections
to help families grow closer to God—and to each other.

🎧 Listen now at **hallow.com/collections/2362**